T0099492

With honesty and humanity, Mary Kudenov describes living in the Alaska you'll never see in travel brochures—a raw place of sketchy neighborhoods and working-class poverty, casual violence and damaged people, loneliness and loss. Yet among those more familiar with heartbreak than happiness, Kudenov locates the dignity of hope, even for herself. *Threadbare* is devastating but quietly beautiful, filled with luminous moments, wry truths, and all the right questions.

—Sherry Simpson, author of *The Way Winter Comes* and *The Dominion of Bears*

The memoiristic arc of *Threadbare: Class and Crime in Urban Alaska* invites comparison to J. D. Vance's *Hillbilly Elegy*, an up-by-the-bootstraps memoir and surprise *N.Y. Times* bestseller as the U.S. suddenly scrambled to rediscover and understand "the working class." Both writers rise from poverty and family wreckage through education, more or less, and hard work. Vance, who earned a law degree at Yale, has a needed story to tell, and, scaffolded by conservative support and mentorship, he gets it told. Kudenov, on the other hand, is a writer first, with the powerful gifts of one born to it, including richly textured prose that moves as easily as light over every imaginable subject and emotive terrain. She demonstrates the most necessary gift for a writer of stature: intellectual inquiry into the world, on behalf of not only her own life, but the lives of those who fill these pages and embody the hardest of questions.

—Linda McCarriston, author of *Eva-Mary* and *Little River*

# THREADBARE

CLASS AND CRIME IN URBAN ALASKA

MARY KUDENOV

Text © 2017 University of Alaska Press

Published by
University of Alaska Press
P.O. Box 756240
Fairbanks, AK 99775-6240

Cover and interior design by Jen Gunderson, 590 Design, fiveninetydesign.com
Cover image by Sara Galletto / EyeEm

Library of Congress Cataloging-in-Publication Data

Names: Kudenov, Mary, author.
Title: Threadbare : class and crime in urban Alaska / by Mary Kudenov.
Other titles: Class and crime in urban Alaska
Description: Fairbanks : University of Alaska Press, 2017. | Includes bibliographical
    references.
Identifiers: LCCN 2017008267 (print) | LCCN 2016058013 (ebook) | ISBN 9781602233409
    (pbk. : alk. paper) | ISBN 9781602233416 (e-book)
Subjects: LCSH: Kudenov, Mary—Homes and haunts. | Kudenov, Mary—Friends and
    associates. | Working class—Alaska. | Alaska—Social life and customs. |
    Alaska—Social conditions.
Classification: LCC PS3611.U32 Z75 2017 (ebook) | LCC PS3611.U32 (print) | DDC
    818/.603—dc23

LC record available at https://lccn.loc.gov/2017008267

*for Seth*

# CONTENTS

# PART ONE

*I need mercy*
*to make life that easy in this world.*
*If not that, I need to harden my edges*
*but mercy is a word*
*that leaves me open instead.*

—*Linda Hogan, "Mercy, the Word"*

# MERCY

I.

My brother Corkey rented the big gray house near the airport, and it was grander than anything I'd lived in, still as cement, quiet as a picture frame. It was quiet because I didn't hear the single-engine planes anymore, rising and falling like giant mosquitoes from the swampy shores of Southeast Alaska. I was quiet, too, during the long stretches when he was away at logging camp or on a construction job. I waited for him with Tracie, my brother's young wife, who would be sending me north to live with my mother as soon as the wild grasses turned to straw and Sears released the Back-to-School catalog.

The voice in my head was transforming into an echo of grownup imperatives: *Put on clothes, something clean that Tracie will like. When you go downstairs, don't tromp.* At the long breakfast table, I sat across from Tracie and asked if my mom had called. When she said no, I asked for Captain Crunch.

"Say please."

"Please. Did she call last night? After I went to bed?"

"Get your elbow off the table. No."

I held my hands still in my lap while she poured the cereal. Someday, I knew, someday I would be a lady, like Baby on *Dirty Dancing*. Even Tracie thought my manners were getting better. Soon nobody would be able to tell I was raised by two teenage boys. I washed my hands before meals and never commented on bodily functions, no matter how funny. I had donned the internal corset of good manners: *Stop talking when you chew; it's gross. Go play outside.*

Somewhere off the airstrip, our cat Bogus hunted for mice in the tall grass. Her kittens played in an old shed that smelled like kerosene and sawdust—my favorite place. It was big enough to hold a small plane and maybe it had once, but in 1988 it was full of old shovels and rusty saws. Spider silk hung from corners and spanned the firewood stacked neatly on the dirt floor.

Sunlight, yellow and hot, fingered in through the cracks in the boards. I sat in the puddles of light, watching Bogus's kittens fight and play. Occasionally they would stop their games and sniff the corners looking for their mom. She didn't care if I held them or named them. Cali. Oatmeal. Charlie. Morris. I could spend hours in that shed. A single strip of sun warmed Cali's fur as she slept in my lap, stretched out like a slinky.

Bogus shot past us on quiet feet, her mouth full of something. She set a live mouse down in the dirt in front of me. I could see its little heart pulse against its ribs, the only movement of its brown body. A scared baby mouse, pulled from the grass. Bogus, was teaching her kittens to hunt. They must. And I knew I shouldn't interfere. It was agony watching the kittens bat him around while he froze in fear. Cali crouched, shook her butt, and pounced.

*Save him,* said the voice.

I grabbed the baby from Cali and held him in the center of my palm. He was bleeding, barely moving. Suffering.

*Just put him out of his misery*, I told myself. *Give him back.*

Oatmeal batted him to Cali. Cali flung him by my feet. It was time to make a deal with myself: if I picked up the mouse and he was still breathing, I would nurse him back to health. I held him right in front of my eyes. His chest was barely moving. I poured my prized white pebbles out of a silver Sucrets tin and put the mouse inside. The kittens gathered at my feet, waiting for my next move. He looked beyond saving. I made another deal with myself: if he was still alive in five minutes, I would give him back, and if he was dead, I would bury him.

I knew enough about the cats to assume they were never going to eat him. It's the hunt that kittens like.

*Dig a hole.*

There was soft ground on the far end of the driveway. Packing a shovel out of the shed would only invite Tracie's attention. Instead,

I used my hands, ripped up the weeds, and dug into the dirt with my nails. The earth was soft but gravelly, just enough soil for the strong wild grasses that grew past my waist.

*It doesn't have to be deep.*

I wanted it to be over with. I ran back to the shed and grabbed the tiny coffin.

*Don't look inside. Just get it over with.*

After, I went inside to wash up, taking time to scrub my black fingernails back to a ladylike pink. Tracie would like that. But the moment I was satisfied that my hands were clean, I realized I never checked to see if the mouse was still breathing when I buried him.

The sun was high, so high that nothing had shadows—not the house or the shed, not even the grass. The consequences of my first act of pity were rooting into me like a weed.

I dug him up and sat back on my ankles looking at the box. Had I buried him alive? Was he still suffering? I couldn't bring myself to look. Instead, I leaned over and pressed my ear to the tin.

*Listen.*

## II.

The next-door neighbor, Mark Andrews, shot more than twenty of his huskies on Mother's Day. The good shots killed, quick and neat. Twelve dogs found alive had to be euthanized later at the animal shelter.

I heard it that night, lying in bed. Bang. Bang. Bang. The shots interrupted my teenage reverie of boys and bikes and summer's-almost-here. The bang rang in my head and rattled through my spine. I told myself not to be scared. *You're almost sixteen years old. People just shoot guns around here.* Bang. Bang-bang. Right next door.

The *Anchorage Daily News* and the *Seward Phoenix Log* reported on it, a big story for sleepy Moose Pass, Alaska. A few months earlier, in January of 1996, troopers found 284 marijuana plants in Mark's home, enough to live on, off the books. Enough to assure a long stay in Seward's Spring Creek Correctional Center. But what neither paper mentioned was that after the bust, the signs went up:

*Free Huskies*. An ad in the classified section. I heard it on the radio in town: *Free Huskies at Mile 29*. By March I could see their rib bones; he fed them only every other day to make the food last.

The neighbors said that Mark walked down to the Moose Pass Inn that night, bought a fifth of Canadian Hunter from the only liquor store in town, and drank it. Sometimes I wonder if he cried. I bet he did. I try not to think about it.

Bang. Moose Pass stirs with the muted ghosts of barking dogs. The whole kennel has gone quiet.

At sixteen years old, I was still a mystery to myself, and I didn't know Mark apart from what I'd heard in town gossip. But I believed something, and it grew out of me like a dandelion: what the papers didn't report, couldn't (because what kind of person can sympathize with the monster that "stacked the dead dogs ten-high like cord wood"?), was that somewhere in that mad, gun-slinging drunkenness, was a sick man ready to skip town and desperate to show one last act of mercy.

## III.

Jade's eyes move in their sockets like flies in a jar. This is not the kind of woman who does one thing at a time. I watch Jade wipe off the desk in the education center with disinfectant and close drawers with the nudge of her knee. A small radio rests in the breast pocket of her scrubs and she has pulled the headphones down to her neck to talk. Pop music blares from the small speakers, and Jade rocks with the beat as she talks and cleans.

Jade's hot-wire energy didn't make me nervous like it once had, like it should have after working in Hiland for two years. *Don't get soft*, I told myself and inched my hand a little closer to the radio that could instantly connect me to the nearest guard. I forced myself to read Jade's dull yellow scrubs, the bold, black font that said PRISONER.

Jade was telling me a story. She said, "She looks like a wolf now. Howls like a wolf. Hair all crazy and shit. She just paces in there, day and night. You know? They haven't let anyone talk to her for like a year."

Jade was talking about another inmate who had been confined to the Solitary Treatment Unit of Hiland Mountain Correctional Center, where I teach remedial math and creative writing. Solitary was the prison inside prison. Prison squared.

"It's fucked," Jade was saying. "They act like she's an animal. She can't even talk to her mom." That really irritated Jade, whose own mother had died less than a year before.

"*No one* is allowed to talk to her? Not even other women in the hole?" I asked, stretching my voice into obvious skepticism.

"Nope," Jade said.

I was thirty years old at the time of this conversation, and the thought of no human contact made me squirm, and I could see that it made Jade squirm too. *No words, no touch, no pity?* I remembered feeling so lonely once that my insides had turned into air and I disappeared inside a big gray house.

"I'm never going back to the hole. Fuck that," Jade continued. "You know that girl?" She was still talking about the Wolf. "She's been in there two years. Every night she cries, and no one will talk to her. So here's what I do: I'm mopping, right? And I know the guard who's working this one day and she's cool; she doesn't look. I'm mopping and mopping and mop right over to her cell. I squat down by the meal slit, like this—"

Jade crouched to demonstrate. With her thick muscular legs and short black hair, she looked like a wild momma panther, might spring any minute.

"I say *Psst. Psst. Come here, girl.* But she's scared of me. She thinks I'm some big, mean dyke. So I say, *no girl—come here. I just want to talk to you. Come here.*" Jade motioned to me like I was the wolf woman, pacing behind the steel bars like a zoo animal.

"I say, *It's okay. It's okay, girl. I just want to say hi. You want me to bring you a book or something? I'll bring you a book.*" Jade delivered the last lines of the story in a high register, like she was talking to a little girl after a nightmare. For one long second, an expression of perfect charity softened her features before they turned back to felon's stone.

At first, each act of humanity I had witnessed in Hiland looked naked and brave. But I began to wonder if they were all around me. I wanted to believe that when people do something bad, horrible even, they do it with misguided benevolence. I took my hand off the radio and leaned into the story. I wanted Jade to say she opened the door for the wolf woman. I wanted the woman to see her mother, to feel the touch of another human being.

"Do you think they will ever let her into open population?" I asked.

Jade stood up, wiped her palms on her thighs, and said, "No. She's wild now."

I'd been holding my breath, and when I finally let it out, I pretended to blow the cotton-tipped seeds from the orb of a dandelion. *Close your eyes. Don't worry about the radio. Inside you're as big as a meadow.* The seeds floated out of the education center and over the razor-wire fences, floated away.

# A HISTORY OF SMOKING

Amber stuffed the hollow stalks of old cow parsnip with dried grass, lit the end, and smoked it like a roll-your-own. We were so young, first or second grade. Our babysitter, Buffy, a brown terrier-poodle mix, investigated nearby bushes but never wandered far. Leaning against the log-sized roots of the Traffic Tree, we pretended to be older, like the big kids who smoked "weeds" out of soda cans here. In the very spot we enjoyed our first cigarette, we'd once watched a game of spin the bottle, secretly observing locked-lip teenagers. We could be ninja quiet in the right circumstances, but there was no need for it that day. We passed the smoke between us like old pros.

Amber's well-worn sweat suit hosted an alphabet collage, A through Z in multiple colors, the white letters yellowing and the knees threadbare. Amber lived next door to me with her father, brother, and sister. I was a little jealous that she had a dad, *and* he was home most of the time, while my mom was often working. Learning my father's name was growing into an obsession, and Amber understood—she had her own mysteries to solve. A couple years before, her mother went out for drinks and never made it back home. She might have been somewhere called Seattle, Amber thought.

Amber held her makeshift cigarette with her whole hand, sucked in as hard as she could, and coughed when she exhaled.

"Does your mom smoke?" she asked when she could talk again.

"Yeah, I guess. I broke all her cigarettes a long time ago, when I was like three," I said. I didn't really want to talk about my mom. I didn't really want to smoke either, yet the fake cigarettes had been my idea. I closed my throat and tilted my head, letting the smoke escape from my open mouth before it got too far inside.

Sunshine fell through the spruce in tiny patches, spotting us with yellow. Buffy, satisfied that the woods were safe, lay down and rested his head on my knee. He smelled like moss and wet dog and I probably did too, sitting as we were on damp ground.

"Did your mom smoke?" I asked to be polite. Amber always wanted to talk about her mom.

"I don't remember," she said.

On nights when my mother didn't come home before I went to bed, I watched HBO with my big brother, Seth. *Children of the Corn*, *Friday the 13th*, *Creepshow*, *Fraggle Rock*. When she did come home, she smelled like pancakes and sausage and fries—the Bamboo Room aroma, a scent that wafts off all diner waitresses. I would sleep in the living room with her just to be near it. If the tooth fairy left quarters, they were sticky with maple syrup. Every day I asked my mother for information about my father, and she pretended not to hear me. Seth told me it was probably Frank, and I understood that was likely the truth, but I needed my mom to say so.

It poured in Southeast Alaska, pennies and frogs and buckets of rain. When our straw-stuffed cow parsnip got too soggy to light, I took Amber to the place I knew only as the old folks home. Frank lived there in an apartment across the hall from my grandfather.

"My mom wants to know if she can have a cigarette," I said when the door opened.

"She does?" He sounded surprised, delighted. We waited in his TV room while he went into the bedroom.

The apartments in Frank's building were for really, really old people, over fifty-five. My grandpa called it the Wrinkle Farm. There were no steps or raised floors, and everything smelled weird. A single brown couch faced a small color television with two round knobs and rabbit ear antennas. The carpet was forest green and hard as tile. My favorite thing about Frank's TV room was a glass-encased stack of paper with a dollar bill on top. He kept it on his coffee table by a candy dish, a cribbage board, and an enormous ashtray. When I was really little, like three, I thought the whole stack was money. I saw Amber eyeing it and the dish of candy, and I felt wise.

Frank came from his room and handed me two packs of Winstons. Amber and I looked at each other, surprised that our plan had worked. It was enough cigarettes to last us until the next year.

"Thanks, Frank."

"Any time, sweetheart. You tell your mom I said *any time*."

❧

Inside my Anchorage apartment twenty years later, a man lies naked on my bed. The sheets and blankets beneath him are still neatly made. We never get under the covers because there is no means to control the temperature. Heat hisses from the furnace at the same rate, regardless of season. It's early in the evening, just past seven, and the relentless light of Alaska's July squeaks in through the sides of my blinds.

The man will never be able to sleep here. He'll never get used to the light and the planes erupting into the sky at the neighboring air force base. Dust from the Glenn Highway seeps in through the window screens. Before he came over, I meticulously wiped gray soot from all the surfaces, knowing that by the next day, it would creep back and he would be gone.

I am not tired, will not try to sleep for many hours. Instead I'm outside enjoying the unhurried setting of the northern sun, scheduled to dip below the horizon around 2:00 a.m. I'm seated atop a milk crate on the second floor walkway, inhaling and exhaling with the slow, practiced breaths of a longtime smoker.

The man's name is unimportant. When I talk about him with my girlfriends, I call him Firefighter. The man before him was the Artist, and before him, Brian (Ex). Firefighter is a decent man, with a job to keep him busy, and by next summer he will have forgotten all about me, or so I tell myself. But I'm not thinking about this while I smoke.

I'm thinking how I resent East Anchorage, loathe the way a bad part of town can suit me so well. The street I live on wakes up after dinner. Grandiose subwoofers punch bass out all night, neighborhood children squeal and scream, military planes roar overhead, and streams of semis whoosh down the highway on the other side of a chain-link fence. This is my place in the small city I moved to five years ago. I breathe the familiar exhaust and feel like I belong.

When the cigarette burns to the butt, I flick it into a bucket and light another. I go hours without smoking for Firefighter because the smell will only make him leave sooner. Although we'll never really know each other, I do feel safer when he's around.

My efficiency is on the top corner of a two-story apartment building in south Mountain View, a notoriously rough neighborhood. The windows face north to the air force base and highway, and west toward downtown. I watch a mother who walks in my direction with her daughter. They have a small dog on a leash, and it excitedly weaves between the gravel of the driveways they walk past and the potholed road they walk on. Many in this part of town rely on bicycles or the bus, yet this street has no sidewalk. The woman catches my eye, sees that I'm watching her, and pulls her daughter a little closer.

The black sedan rolls soundlessly behind them, but my eyes are all for the pup, a Scottish terrier mix. He's on a leash that connects to the mother. He's spry and bouncy, thrilled to be out with his people. The little girl, maybe five, stays much closer to the woman. Pup darts slightly into the road and the car has no time to stop. Both right wheels bump, bump, and halt.

They have all reached the intersection by my apartment. The woman and child stand perfectly still. She reaches down to grip her daughter's arm, cementing the child in place. The passenger side window of the sedan rolls down, and the woman says something I can't hear to the driver. By now the child has begun to process that the other end of the leash is still, that something isn't right.

"Snoopy?" the girl asks. "Snoopy?" A note of hysteria enters her question. The woman drops the leash, lifts her child into her arms and turns in a run up the street.

I am also trying to process what I witnessed, life and death in the span of a minute. The black car inches forward slightly, and I hear myself yelling, "Don't you move," and run down the steps to cross the intersection and reach the sedan, thinking I might prevent a hit and run. I try to memorize his license plate. Closer to the vehicle, I see that the sedan is an unmarked police car and the man behind the wheel is in a uniform.

"What do you want?" he says.

"I'm sorry. I didn't realize you were an officer. I just wanted to make sure you didn't leave." When I say it, I realize how ridiculous it sounds. So what if he wasn't a cop? What if he did leave? But the officer seems not to really hear me. His hands are still on the steering wheel and he looks straight ahead, jaw clenched.

"You have to keep them off the road!" he says. "You don't put them on a leash and then let them run in front of cars. I didn't even *see* him. I didn't even see the leash." I note his dark hair and good skin, the crispness of his uniform. He seems to want me to understand where the fault lies. Perhaps he's talking to himself, or practicing how he will report this.

My pity shifts from the little girl to the officer and finally to myself for having to witness his shame. I throw my cigarette butt down and stomp on it, realize self-consciously that I just littered, and stoop down to pick it back up.

"The dog should have been walking on the inside," he says. But we both know the child was walking on the inside where her mother could better keep her from running into the street.

I walk around the car. The dog isn't bleeding; he just looks a little misshapen. I reach down and touch his still body, his warm fur that is as soft as winter fleece. Just two minutes ago I was on my deck smoking, while Snoopy filled his senses with the smells and textures of our neighborhood, leash attached as securely as a training wheel. *What am I doing here?* I wonder. My breath shortens to a pant, and I try to swallow down a panic attack. The cop looks at me curiously. I've been touching the dead dog for too long.

A few minutes later I push open the door to my apartment. Firefighter covers his head with a pillow and says, "I don't know how you sleep in here with all this light."

"I like it," I say. "I don't know how you can sleep so early." I attempt to wash the cigarette smell off my hands and slide back onto the bed with him. I rest my head on his chest but the heat is too much. My bed and my apartment are just the right size for me and my cat. Firefighter leaves within the hour.

I make myself a glass of ice water and lie down on the floor where I can't smell Firefighter's spicy shampoo on my pillow. My breath shortens again. The little girl is a still frame, secured in her mother's arms. For the rest of my memory they will be heading home, and Snoopy's soft body, warm forever. I have split my mind in two: I'm in the sedan replaying the scene, asking myself if I've really been paying attention; I'm a lonely woman laid out on the floor, panting, because it's hot and bright and excruciatingly empty.

&

Buffy and I walked my brand-new birthday bicycle to the hill in front of the old folks home around 5:00 a.m. It didn't feel early. The tireless light of Alaska's June meant the sun never really set anyway.

My bike was *so* cool. It had pink tassels on the handlebars and a big basket situated behind the banana seat. I had yet to success- fully ride anything without training wheels, but I imagined myself pedaling all over town (or at least all the way to Amber's grandma's house) with a basket full of daisies and kittens, the wind ruffling the tassels at my hands. My brother Corkey had spent hours holding the seat and running behind me the night before, trying to keep me up straight, but every attempt ended in a crash. We finally gave up, defeated and cranky, me in tears—not for how much I crashed, but from embarrassment.

That morning I resolved to ride all the way around Deishu Drive before Corkey woke up. We lived in a horseshoe-shaped neighbor- hood set off from another road. My mother was working-poor and proud. Not once did she apply for welfare or assistance, even when we likely needed it. However, she was comfortable securing a rent- to-own modular home on Deishu Drive, available to single parents and low-income families. It was a leg up, but she was still paying her own way. My grandfather, like Frank, lived two minutes away, in low-income senior housing.

No one was awake yet, so I wasn't worried about people seeing me fall. I mounted my bike at the top of the hill and put my feet on both pedals, which is where they remained as I tipped over and slammed the side of my arm and leg into the asphalt. This won't work, I thought. I'm not even going anywhere. At least when my brother was pushing me I was moving when I crashed. That seemed better somehow. I stood back up, gripped the handlebars, and slid one leg over the seat to mount it. Maybe if I push off with my other foot, I'll at least be able to go down the hill a little before I wreck.

Launching the bike forward with the foot still connected to the ground, I managed to get both feet on the pedals and the wheels rolling, but I wasn't going straight. I veered off the road, smashing into a car parked in front of the old folks home. I felt Buffy's tongue on the back of my neck.

"Go home, boy!" I said.

Buffy loitered at the top of the hill, unwilling to leave me alone. My hands were bleeding when I pulled myself up against my bike. Frank had opened his curtains and stood at the window watching. Shame burnt up my neck and spread across my cheeks.

"Get out of here!" I yelled toward Buffy.

I was resolved. I walked the bike back up to the top of the hill and tried again. And again, and again. I didn't need a father or even a mother, I told myself, yet I was acutely aware that Frank watched. Some other pain superseded the sting of road rash, pushing me on. The feeling snapped into place like a puzzle piece, and my body learned what it had to do to keep me upright, to balance.

Perhaps this was the first time I had focused my will. It is the first time I remember. I pretended to ignore Frank and the other old people who had come outside to the common deck with their morning coffee. I pedaled fast around the block all that day and all that summer. Each morning Frank watched for me, leaning out of his window with his big mug of coffee in one hand and a cigarette in the other. Some mornings he sat on the common deck with his neighbors. Once he said, loud enough for me to hear, "That's my daughter, you know." *Mmmm-hmmm*, said some other old person, like they didn't believe him either.

❧

Lou pulls himself from a brown Lincoln, cane first. I sit on the top step smoking and journaling and drinking tea. Lou lives two doors down from me in number 5. Technically, he is the building manager, which means he collects the rent for the landlord once a month. No one can really manage this building, but his presence reminds tenants that *someone* owns this property. In theory, that should keep the parties quieter and windows unbroken.

Lou shuffles around the other cars, and I wait until he arrives at the stairs to offer help. With a cane in one hand and groceries in the other, he won't be able to hold the railings. One of Lou's legs is a few inches longer than the other, and he's old enough that he can no longer pretend he doesn't need help now and again. Still, he's proud and I don't offer to carry things until he reaches the stairs.

Lou has thinning white hair, missing teeth, yellow skin, and the exploding nose of an old alcoholic. He's been sober for twenty years, maybe less. The lines in his face and the spots on his hands are telltale signs of a man who lived hard for a time and lost everything more than once.

"Thanks, sweetheart," he says when I grab his bags. "You're a good girl."

I'm a good girl by Lou's standards—I work, pay my rent, go to school. I don't smoke meth, snort coke, shoot dope. I've never been in prison, never even been in jail. I'm pink-cheeked and chubby and helpful, not like some of the sunken-eyed, skinny women who wander in and out of the downstairs apartments, always asking for a dollar or a smoke or a ride.

Lou and I became acquainted in the mornings when I would smoke on the deck where he shaved willow branches into canes. He's straightforward and warm but not nosy. Trustworthy. He loves wood, shapes it deftly with hands bent and arthritic. I wonder that he doesn't get hurt or robbed—the landlord doesn't accept checks, only cash and money orders, so Lou is vulnerable around the first of the month. Also, he never locks his door when he is home. When I go over to play cribbage, he hollers to "just come on in, sweetheart," like it's only ever sweethearts who come knocking.

I lean on Lou's doorframe, holding his bags while he limps up the stairs. Today he sounds winded, and he's looking especially jaundiced.

"How you doing, Lou? You had lunch yet?" I ask.

"According to the doc, I might make it through the day," he says. Lou unlocks his door and I walk in behind him, setting his shopping bags on the counter. His efficiency layout is the mirror opposite of mine. Boxes fill the area that acts as a living room and bedroom.

Lou's apartment is almost packed up. I ask when he's leaving. He plans to go to Arizona for the summer, to visit his daughter one last time. Over the winter, Lou's doctor discovered his liver was failing, giving him an indeterminate amount of time to finish his projects and make amends with his estranged children. That's all that matters now, he told me, this wish to see his daughter, to be forgiven.

"Cowboy is coming over later tonight to load up all my boxes and take me to the airport." Cowboy is the maintenance man, an old friend of Lou's and another old bachelor type who will be moving in and taking over the building manager title.

I don't like saying good-bye, and I don't want to make a scene that would just embarrass Lou, so I give him a quick hug and spend the rest of the day trying not to be on the deck at the same time as him.

℘

The summer of 1990, weeks before Frank died of a heart attack, I asked my aunt to tell me, once and for all, who my father was. I was almost ten years old and found the not-knowing totally unfair, I explained.

"Mary Beth," she said, "I already told you who your father is, as has your brother. It *is* Frank. You know that!" she said it with finality, closing the subject. I would not be able to ask her the same thing in a different way and get a different answer.

*Why won't they just tell me the truth?* I thought. Frank was clearly too *old* to be my father. He was at least a hundred and something. He was potbellied and bald, had big cow eyes and floppy jowls. He even wore suspenders. Like my grandpa. The hard candies on his coffee table were so stale they picked up in clumps that had melted together. He didn't even have Tang on his counter. He couldn't be anyone's dad.

But while I thought of these things, I grew aware of something else. It was like that moment in a dream when you begin to question how it is that you're flying or how a house made of Play-Doh doesn't just crumble: if Frank wasn't my dad, why was I always visiting him? How come I couldn't remember the first time I met him? Why did he open the door to the hallway whenever I visited my grandfather in the old folks home?

And so I found myself at the door to Frank's apartment, curious and horrified when he opened to my knocking. I must have looked a sight: a quiet child in his doorway, contemplating him with fearful and serious eyes. I was trying my hardest to picture him as my dad. This just can't be, I concluded. I forced myself to say the words, "Hi, Daddy," to gauge his response.

Frank looked delighted. His enormous eyebrows lifted; in fact, his whole face changed, unwrinkled. "Well, come here then, sweetheart," he said. He opened his arms and waited for me to run into them. The moment was eerily dissonant. I couldn't reach the man who wanted to hug his daughter and never would. I clung instead to feeling rejected.

This was the last time I saw my dad's face and the first time I split myself in two—I was the girl who smoked in the woods, wistful for a father, and I was the girl who taught herself to stay upright and told herself she didn't give a damn.

When I could move again, I ran down the hallway with the hard green carpet and out the door.

❧

"'Kate and I would sometimes meet after work at the Pilsen dressed in proper business clothes and still feeling both a little self-conscious and glamorous, as if we were impostors wearing disguises,'" Peter reads. I reach up and flip the lamp off, burrowing farther into the covers.

"How long is this story?"

"Just a couple pages. You'll like it. The ending is lovely," he says.

*Lovely?*

Stuart Dybek is tonight's writer. Last night Peter read "Cathedral" and choked up when the narrator started drawing with his eyes closed. I'm not used to men who cry when they're sober.

"Is it happy?" I ask.

"The ending? Yes, it lifts off the page."

*Lifts off the page?*

It has to be happy. Last week, when he read "The Things They Carried," I cried to the point of hiccups after he hung up. After my brother Seth died, I stopped watching drama and horror. I stopped reading anything I couldn't buy in a grocery store. But I'm not ready to tell Peter that. Right now it's best that he thinks of me as a girl who likes happy endings.

This slow speed of Peter is hard for me to understand. By the end of our third date, I was perfectly perfumed and ready to finish the evening inside. I stood pressed against my front door, panting from the silkiest, most thorough kiss I'd ever experienced in the open air.

"Come inside," I breathed into his ear.

"I don't know . . ." He trailed a finger down my neck. "I don't know if it's the right time. I have to think about it."

"There's nothing to think about but this. Right now," I entreated. He tipped back his head and laughed, pulling far enough away that I could no longer feel his warmth. "I'll call you when I get home."

That was the night of our first story.

As he reads I listen sometimes to the story, sometimes to the sound of his voice. My cat curls into the crook of my arm, and Dybek's leading man falls in love. "'This time, seeing her reflection hovering ghost-like upon an imaginary Prague was like seeing a future from which she had vanished. I knew I'd never meet anyone more beautiful to me.'"

"Hey, Peter," I interrupt. "I have to ask you something serious."

"Umm. Okay," he says, sounding hesitant.

"Are you ever going to put out?"

He laughs for a minute. "Yes, Mary. Just listen to the story."

Outside, a winter storm pushes wisps of snow into the corners of the windowpane. I can't hear any cars on the highway or planes overhead, and I might be able to fall asleep earlier than normal. I wish I had the courage to ask Peter if he can sleep with the phone by his pillow, with the line still open. I wish that I could reach across this loneliness and find an anchor.

"'It was as if I were standing on that platform, with my school books and a smoke,'" Peter's voice spills out and in. He's trying to summon the courage to tell me something of himself as well. "'I stood almost outside of time simply waiting for a train, and I thought how much I'd have loved seeing someone like us streaming by.'"

❧

It was the last summer I would spend in my Mountain View shoebox apartment. Things were going to get better soon, I was going to graduate, marry Peter, and move to a safer neighborhood, but I didn't know that. I woke up late on a rare day off, set a pot of coffee to brew, and grabbed my journal. My favorite breakfast nook was the dirty green milk-crate seat I kept just below my wind chimes.

The apartment building had never looked so tidy. Cowboy was mowing the patches of grass beside the parking lot and picking up the litter that accumulated in the driveway each night. Even the rosebush, grown so wild it had crept into the visitor parking spot, was clipped and neat, reined in at the base by a brick hedge. Cowboy and I had built it together the week before with materials he found on one of his proud dumpster-diving excursions.

I let the smell of cut grass, exhaust from the highway, and the fresh air underneath all of it fill my senses for a second before I lit up. That cigarette was to be bittersweet enjoyment. It was time to quit smoking. The day before, Peter had stopped taking drags and asked for his own. At first he would just join me on the deck while I smoked, to keep me company. But things had progressed, and I felt I was making a mess of him.

We had been dating for almost a year. I couldn't explain to Peter (or understand myself) why smoking was excusable in my case but horrifying in his. I didn't know what I thought of myself, but the truth was all around me in a crime-ridden neighborhood, my glazed-doughnut breakfast, the waffle-waitress jobs. I knew I didn't want to be a bad influence on a good man. Maybe this was love. I decided I would relish that last pack and quit a habit I had fostered since childhood. Even if it meant worrying over the cost of nicotine patches or several months of withdrawal.

Cowboy had turned off the lawnmower and was crawling on his hands and knees in a patch of grass. This was awkward to watch: Cowboy was tall, maybe six foot two, had thick glasses and an un-groomed gray-and-white beard that blasted off from his face in all directions. He covered his male-pattern baldness with a crusty ball cap. He usually wore paint-stained work jeans and flannel, even on warm days. I'd come to think of the whole look as standard, blue-collar Anchorage. He kept a set of tools on his person—screwdrivers and pliers in his breast pocket, hammer in a belt loop, screws and washers in his pants pockets.

"You looking for rocks?" I called down to him.

"No, ma'am." He stood, walked up the steps, and handed over two four-leaf clovers. He then pulled a pack of Marlboro filters out of his overstuffed pockets and lit up. "I'm a lucky man," he said.

"Why do you say that?"

"Did you know I grew up on a farm? That's why they call me Cowboy."

"What's your real name?" I asked.

"David Boyton. Long story short: I got kicked by a cow right here." He pulled off his cap and pointed to the front of his bald spot. It looked like every other bald spot to me.

"So now you have an affinity with cows?" I asked.

"No. But I'm lucky. I can go down there right now and pick you ten four-leaf clovers with my eyes closed."

"Is that right? With your eyes closed?" Cowboy could make himself the hero of any anecdote.

"Yep." He reached into his pants pocket and pulled out a cluster of clovers, holding open his hand in front of me. All had four leaves.

"How do I know you haven't been collecting those all morning?" I said.

"Hold this." He handed me his lit cigarette and stuffed the four-leaf clovers back into his pockets. He went to a different patch of grass directly in front of the parking lot. "Watch me now," he said. With his eyes closed he put out his hands and started walking in circles like a zombie. After a second, he stopped, hands out still, and dropped to his knees. I saw him pluck grass but couldn't tell if his eyes were still closed. He pushed himself up and came back, taking his still-lit cigarette from my hand and replacing it with four more four-leaf clovers.

"You can keep those too," he said.

I looked at the clovers, thinking he must have done some sleight-of-hand maneuver and grabbed some that were in his pocket. But the clovers weren't crushed or wrinkled. I slipped them into my journal with the first two he'd given me.

"When I was a boy I got kicked by a cow, and it knocked me out. When I came to I was lying in a patch of clovers. Ever since, I can feel for them," he said.

"What does it feel like?"

"I don't know. Maybe like electricity or something. But it's not just that. I can feel when I'm going to get lucky."

What is so lucky about Cowboy? I asked myself. Almost sixty years old, living alone in a tiny apartment in a bad neighborhood, kicked in the head as a kid, and now he *feels* lucky. But I wanted to believe him more than I wanted to be cynical. I liked his good outlook, and now I had a journal full of lucky charms.

"Thanks for the clovers, Cowboy. I need all the luck I can get. I think I'm going to try to quit smoking. After this pack."

"Oh yeah? Well, if I could quit drinking, you can quit smoking," he said.

"How long you been sober?"

"Fifteen years," he said, then changed his mind. "Maybe five. It took me a few tries. It doesn't take luck, though. It takes balls. Big balls and hard work."

"So it's a lot like everything else."

"Pretty much."

Cowboy tossed his cigarette in the can and sat on the top step, looking outward or inward, I couldn't tell. It was a good silence, an easy silence. I smelled the coffee brewing in my apartment, and a sweeter smell wafting up from the rosebush. I'd read that the sense of smell is the first thing a body recovers in nicotine withdrawal. I arranged the remaining clovers into my journal and wondered if I could capture that luck—the essence of clover, green and fresh, pushing up and up and into summer.

# NOTES FROM A BALTIC AVENUE

Brian, my soon-to-be ex, was crouched in the kitchen of our basement apartment, trying to coax a shrew out from under the refrigerator. Our gray tabby, Basil, had sensed the change coming. As we had emptied shelves of books and cupboards of pans and plates, she hunted, diplomatically bringing home peace offerings on my behalf.

Have a bird. A mouse. A dead squirrel.

I pulled into the driveway, ready to gather Basil and the last of my belongings. I didn't have a place lined up yet, but I wouldn't have felt much better if I did. I considered spending the summer with my mother. She lived in a town so small, so sweet, that the K–8 elementary school class sent her sympathy cards when her husky died of old age. She still called Anchorage "The City," and she said it with a capital C, even though the population had yet to reach three hundred thousand.

Basil would have liked my hometown. It was green and wooded, brimming with wild things. The town monument was a waterwheel that spun a sharpening stone, and beside that a hand-painted sign read, "Moose Pass is a peaceful little town. If you have an axe to grind, do it here."

I had an axe to grind: Brian had told me that he wanted to start seeing a red-headed woman who was closer to his age and wore her hair in braided pigtails. Her name was Deirdre, as in *Deirdre of Sorrows*. She didn't want kids, because she already had a son.

Brian would never marry me, but he would help me pack.

When I opened the door to our apartment, Basil shot out on spry cat feet and stopped at the top of the stairs, tail twitching, ears back, looking for something to kill.

❧

I needed an affordable place, the kind of apartment that didn't have rules about smoking or pets. I drove east, toward the Chugach Mountains, with Basil nervous beside me in the passenger seat. Bart, the landlord, was to meet us at his south Mountain View apartment complex. He offered a "moving-in bonus"—a piece of paper saying he had collected a $450 security deposit, when in fact, he never would. Presumably, this meant I would receive a gift of $450 upon moving out.

Taku Drive ran alongside a chain-link fence that separated the residential street from the Glenn Highway, the road that led north to the Alaska Range. Denali, the state's most famous mountain, was out there somewhere, wrapped in fog and pulling tourists northward toward some ideal Alaska that they perhaps read about in an adventure magazine. While the promise of a mountain view might have sounded romantic to a visitor, mountains were the common backdrop. It was the foreground that spoke to the neighborhood. Plastic soda bottles, fast food wrappers, and malt beer cans lined the road. I pulled into the driveway of the apartment complex, where a tall man leaned against the driver's side door of the "rebuilt, 1996, green Ford Taurus" he'd given me as a landmark.

Bart was a handsome thirtysomething with John Kennedy Jr. looks: dark hair and bright green eyes minus the dapper quality. He walked toward me, hand extended. Not bothering with small talk, he launched into an explanation of the trash in the parking spaces: "This is all getting cleaned up tomorrow." He indicated the driveway and the yard with a hand's sweep. "I've got one of the Russians coming over to mow the lawn."

"The Russians?"

"Yes, ma'am," he said, his molasses voice warm with used-car-salesman ethos. "I've got some Russians working for me on an exchange program. They're great. It's all on the books. You'll like them."

The Craigslist ad Bart had posted didn't include any photographs or details that acknowledged the building's general disrepair—a broken window in one of the basement units, postal boxes missing doors, dumpster overflowing with loose trash. A piece of cylindrical glass glinted under the tire of my truck. I bent down for a closer look.

"Is that a crack pipe?"

"Damn it!" Bart fake-yelled. "I told them to pick this crap up." He explained that no one wanted to pick up the drug paraphernalia because other tenants didn't want anyone to think it was theirs. "I've got one problem tenant that I'm trying to get rid of, but I have to do everything by the books. We do everything by the books around here."

"Right," I said.

"How about I pick this up and you go look at your new apartment?" he said, slipping the key into my hand. "Top of the stairs. Number 3."

The efficiency's formerly blond wooden floors were gray with wear and water damage, and the linoleum in the kitchen was torn in several places. An ancient refrigerator leaked Freon and the smell overwhelmed the small space. I walked to the center and turned in a slow circle, making a note of what it would take to make the place livable: blinds, bleach, a throw rug or two. I would stick it out until I graduated or found something nicer for the same price. I told myself either was possible and to look on the upside, to find something to like. The walls consisted mostly of windows. The light would be a refreshing change. The windows faced Elmendorf Air Force Base and in time, I reassured myself, I would get used to the boom of the jets.

In the parking lot, Bart made a show of gathering trash and stacking it beside the full dumpster. I leaned out of the apartment door and yelled, "I'll take it."

"Great! I'll send one of the Russians over tomorrow to pick up the rent. Cash only, okay? I just can't take checks. I've been burned too many times." He wiped his hands on shopworn khakis and waved good-bye.

~

After hours of scrubbing and unpacking, I pulled Basil onto my lap for a cuddle. She struggled free and sat with her back to me, staring at the door. She wanted to chase bugs and eat grass, but I didn't want to let her outside with the highway so near.

"I don't like it here either," I said to her turned back. The breakup was a stew of hollowness and stress hormones. I'd lost the person who'd become not just my romantic partner, but the man who paid half the bills and struggled alongside me. Never mind that he was an alcoholic, often unkind, and I could barely tolerate the smell of him— he was the one, I was certain, and I lost him. I was a single woman living alone with my cat. And poor. I was uninsured in the days before the Affordable Care Act and spent almost half of my income paying out-of-pocket for medication I'd needed since childhood. I hoped that college would lead to something more lucrative than a waitressing career, something with health insurance and paid sick days, but there was no guarantee. I knew how close I was to a future like my mother's: a lifetime of working minimum wage jobs up into her seventies and still going. But I didn't have her health. I wouldn't yet call the girl in that apartment an adult, but I understood I was responsible for myself; nobody was going to sweep in and save me from an uncomfortable life. To make ends meet, I would need to stay put.

Traffic from the Glenn, police sirens, and aircraft kept me awake long into the night. I was nostalgic for the tidiness and safety of my childhood home. When it finally got dark enough for the orange streetlights to spill in through the undressed window, I laid down on the used mattress I'd bought the day before. I didn't have sheets yet, and the mattress smelled faintly of moss, a smell that reminded me of Moose Pass. I inhaled the familiar scent and told myself it was soothing.

~

Chelsea and I smoked side-by-side on matching green milk crates. She had moved into number 2 a year earlier, and our balcony habit made us fast friends. She didn't look like a smoker. She had a round

Madonna face and a little frame swimming in big curves. With her porcelain-clear skin and lustrous blonde hair, it was no surprise to hear a strange man yell up to her, "Hey, gurrrrrl!" as he drove by in a car thumping with bass.

Chelsea was a skilled maintenance woman. I called her when I had plumbing or electrical problems, or when I needed my oil changed or help with a flat tire. Her husband, John, was jumping out of planes somewhere above Afghanistan, and his tour wasn't scheduled to end for several months. They had married when John last came home. The cigarette Chelsea smoked was the last one she'd have for several months.

"I'm pregnant," she said.

"Congratulations. Are you sure?"

"I took three tests this morning." She inhaled slowly, eyes closed, and let smoke out in a long, even breath. "They can't all be wrong." The late Alaska sunset gave her features a pink hue. She looked like a painting. "I don't know what to do. We're always so damn broke. And his parents are Mormon."

"Is that bad?"

"No. But they'll probably think this is why we married. Not the best impression."

The music of an ice cream truck drew near. It was close to midnight, but children from the neighboring building raced toward the sound.

"How much you wanna bet there's a pedophile clown driving that truck?" I joked.

"How much you wanna bet he's not just selling ice cream?" she countered.

Taku Drive rests just outside of Mountain View, once considered Anchorage's worst neighborhood before city council committees "cleaned up" around the business districts. But gun crimes and prostitution never went away; they crept into surrounding areas, making our street the dark underbelly of the former underbelly. The first month in my apartment I had called the police often, any time I heard gunshots or arguing, but they seldom came.

"I hate to say this, but if you're going to have this baby, you really need to move."

"I think we'll move back to Wyoming," she said, stubbing her cigarette out on the side of an old coffee can. "I need to be able to count on having water and electricity."

Periodically the water or gas shut off. Once, when the electric company had turned off the lights, I called and begged for power to be restored for tenants who had diligently paid their utilities-included rent. In his most buttery voice, Bart later explained that his accountant had paid the bills with the wrong credit card, again.

Chelsea said goodnight. I stayed on the deck for another cigarette, wondering who would do the maintenance after she moved to Wyoming. Who would help me shovel snow? Who would clean up the litter after the bank finally took the building from Bart and his Russians? And who would move into the apartment next door?

⁌

One year later, Saturday, 10:00 p.m. I was a thousand words into a fifteen-pager due the following Monday. I had an evening shift the next day and needed to boogie on the homework. Basil curled up on my pillow, likely dreaming of the good old days when I used to let her outside to kill things. The place looked good and smelled like a fresh pot of coffee. I had torn up the dirty linoleum, reworked the original wood floors with a belt sander, and picked a cherry varnish. The new landlord did not reimburse me for the materials. Still, the apartment finally felt like mine.

I couldn't focus. Deng Ba Dang was home from a job on the North Slope and was partying with his payday friends. Something slammed against my kitchen wall and rattled the clock. Raucous laughter and generic drunk sounds echoed throughout the building. I stomped to the kitchen and pounded the wall.

They pounded back.

I had liked Deng when he first moved into Chelsea's old apartment, or at least I really liked his name, Deng Ba Dang; the phonetic pop of it thrilled me. *Deng Ba Dang. Deng Ba Dang.* The name bounced around your mouth. He even laughed when he said it out loud. He was a tall Sudanese man who smiled often, his white teeth flashing against his dark skin. He was quiet at first, seldom had company, but this changed once he passed the citizenship test and accepted a job cleaning asbestos out of old buildings on the North Slope where most remote communities are dry. He binge drank whenever he came home.

I checked the locks on my door before going back to my desk. We never locked our doors in Moose Pass, and I often forgot to in Anchorage. After a few minutes of unproductive work, I heard Deng knocking.

"Sarah," he slurred, "open the door."

"Name's not Sarah!" I said. I'd corrected this many times, but I looked like a Sarah to him. I grabbed my pepper spray and opened the door. Deng spilled into my kitchen. He used my shoulders to steady himself and kept his hands there after regaining his balance.

"Don't touch me," I said. He removed his hands but stayed uncomfortably close. I kept the door open so he would understand he was welcome to leave quickly. Basil alerted to the fresh air and looked like she wanted to run for it.

"You give me a ride to get beer, Sarah," he said. Deng had graduated past broken English but was not yet fluent. He asked questions without modals.

"Are you asking if I *can* give you a ride to the liquor store?" I felt his beer breath on my forehead.

"Yes, you *can*?"

"I don't want to, Deng. I'm doing homework." I put my hand on his chest and pushed him back toward the doorway. "Watch your step." I closed the door as soon as his face cleared it and headed back to the computer. Deng seemed harmless, but I was afraid of the predatory way his drunken friends looked at unaccompanied women. They stood blocking my door when I came home, forcing me to interact.

The work went well for a couple hours after Deng left. Party sounds muffled into the background noise of cars on the highway and the growling boiler. Around midnight, my door burst open and one of Deng's friends, a stocky man who looked to be in his late thirties or early forties, stood in my kitchen with a can of beer in his hand. He froze. I froze. I had forgotten to lock the door after Deng came over. I grabbed the pepper spray on my desk, but adrenaline muddled my brain, and I couldn't understand how to maneuver the safety feature in order to make the can work.

"Get the fuck out! Get out!" I screamed, my voice shrill and silly sounding. The man smiled. He said something, but his accent was too thick.

"What?" Behind him the door wasn't closed all the way. *If I scream really loud someone might hear me and do something*, I thought.

"Bang. You bang? Me?" he asked, laughing.

"You're asking me to bang you? I don't understand." He laughed at this too and put his arms up and started backing toward the door. Suddenly, I understood what he was asking me to do.

"I'm going to Mace your fucking eyes out. Asshole!" At this, he recognized anger and left quickly. After a few minutes of waiting on hold for the police, I hung up the phone and stomped over to Deng's door.

"I want to talk to you, Deng!" I yelled through the door. In a chorus, his friends oohed him, as though he were in trouble with the teacher. He stumbled out and gave me a sheepish smile.

"This isn't funny, Deng. If I had a gun, I would have shot your friend. My door is not open to you." I pointed at my closed door to emphasize the point. His smile dropped suddenly, and I thought I was finally getting through to him.

"I know, Sarah," he said. "I drink too much."

⟜

It was not quite October, two years after I had moved in. Leaves lay in brown piles along Taku Drive. I watched public television in the early evening, procrastinating on homework. It was already dark outside. At that time of year, light and dark unfold in even-keeled twelve-hour increments. I felt my life balancing out too. I didn't miss Brian anymore. I worked and studied and slept in late when I could. Basil was fat and as happy as she could get without a live rodent in her mouth. She stretched out on the loveseat, belly-up beside me, willing me to rub her tummy like a dog.

I answered a knock at the door and was surprised to see Lindy Rae, the new landlord's emancipated seventeen-year-old daughter. "Can I come in?" she asked.

Rae sashayed through the open door on high-heel boots that stopped just before her skinny, bare knees. A short skirt rode high up her thighs as she sat. She lifted a gray fedora hat from her head, set it on the back of the couch, and scooped Basil into her lap.

"I love your cat!" she said.

I waited for Rae, as she preferred to be called, to make a pitch. During her first night on Taku Drive, she had invited herself to my door and asked me to buy her alcohol. I had shut the door without answering, and, without missing a beat, she moved on to the next door. Deng was happy to make a pretty new friend.

"Aren't you cold in that skirt?" I asked.

"No." She giggled. I probably sounded like an old woman to her. "Do you like it?"

"It kind of looks like something a stripper would wear," I said, compelled toward honesty.

"Perfect! I'm going to Fantasies tonight to apply for a job." Fantasies was a strip club about a mile down the Glenn Highway.

"Don't you have to be eighteen?"

"It's my birthday." She said it with a flat voice, like it disappointed her. She stroked Basil softly. Her overtly sexual clothing made her look like a vulnerable little girl. Her eyes welled.

"Are you okay?"

"Yes. Well, no. Someone broke all of my windows last night and tore up my apartment," she said. I asked her if they took anything. She said they hadn't, but she thought they were looking for a gun she had found in her ceiling when she first moved in.

A locksmith and his girlfriend had lived in Rae's apartment before her father bought the building. They were polite and quiet and kept mostly to themselves. I didn't understand why Rae's dad had evicted them. The day they moved, the locksmith vented to me while he packed his van. I was smoking on the deck and came down to help him carry a sofa to the parking lot.

"Evict the black man and move your seventeen-year-old daughter in? I'm not stupid," he said. It was a fair point. He paid his rent, which was the only rule you didn't break in a place like ours.

I had seen the locksmith's van around the area, but I'd assumed he just hadn't moved very far. I offered to call the police and tell them. "You know, I didn't think he was a bad guy. Can you just give him back his gun?"

"I already gave it to the cops. Besides, I don't think that's what he wants. There was some other stuff."

"Oh? What kind of stuff?"

"Drugs."

"I'm guessing you didn't give that to the cops. That's probably why he keeps coming around, Rae. He wants his *stuff* back."

Rae looked like she didn't want to leave my couch, like she didn't want to get a job at Fantasies. She looked scared. What was her dad thinking? I knew he was a former alcoholic because Lou, an old man who lived a couple doors down, was his sponsor and had told me as much. Lou had also mentioned that Rae's parents hadn't been sober for much of her childhood. Some would say Rae wasn't a child anymore, but she wasn't ready to live alone. Not there. She was so desperate for attention that she'd eagerly wander into the unknown, unarmed and barely clothed.

"It doesn't matter anyway. My dad's evicting me," she said. Apparently Rae had broken the golden rule and not paid her rent. "He's such an asshole." She gazed blankly ahead, the only movement her slender fingers kneading Basil's fur.

"Just be careful," I said, ridiculously. What eighteen-year-old is careful? But I sensed a future for Rae where nothing turns out well and I think she felt it too.

౿

A few nights later, I woke to police sirens at 3:00 a.m. and lay in bed listening to radios and voices for forty-five minutes before curiosity finally coaxed me outside. Flashing red-and-blue lights blended with the orange glow of the streetlamp. A blanket wrapped tightly around my bare legs, I squatted to talk to a few of Rae's friends who stood below the balcony.

"Is someone getting arrested?" I asked, noting an array of cleavage and thongs, pants that needed pulling up. All across the parking lot, police officers were interviewing teenagers. The group below me had finished talking to the officers who, even in the dark, appeared irritated.

A skeletal brunette looked up at me, the black bags under her eyes so pronounced that I wondered if the cause was meth, lack of sleep, or mascara build-up. Pockmarks encased her mouth and nose and she moved in the jerky fashion I'd come to associate with hard drug users. *It's meth*, I thought.

The boy beside her tightened his arms across his chest. He looked young, probably still a teen, but drunk and surly, a budding alpha male. He gave me one of those what's-it-to-you looks that teenage boys fling around.

"My friend here," he pointed to the brunette, "was just chillin' on the trunk and some *motherfucker* got his panties all up in a twist and called the *fucking* cops, and they *think* she was getting kidnapped or some shit." He said this loud enough for the police to hear, emphasizing certain words to make his point. The brunette rolled her eyes and looked appropriately churlish.

"You were just sitting on the trunk of the car? Why would anyone call the cops about that?" I asked her.

"No, she was *in* the trunk," the boy said for her.

"Why was she *in* the trunk?"

"I don't fucking know. She wanted to be. Why you trippin'?" He scowled, pulling his low-hanging pants up by the crotch. His hand lingered there a moment.

What I wanted to say was "Really? You have to touch your genitals right now? Nobody wants to see that." But the day before, I'd spotted an empty box of .38 shells beneath the stairs.

Let the punk be a punk, I told myself.

When Rae's dad bought the building, he'd given me a card with his business motto spelled out in bold italics: *Safe, Affordable Housing*. I tossed my cigarette into the Folgers can and let the punk's question roll around my head. Why was I tripping?

When the last police car pulled away from the parking lot and Rae's friends dispersed, I slipped back into the relative protection of my apartment. The night had stretched into morning, and traffic whooshed past the chain-link fence that divided Taku Drive from the highway. I lay in bed wondering how many fences kept me and the people in my building in low-rent neighborhoods. There were so many unfulfilled needs, for good parents, education, treatment programs, decent wages. When the community task forces "cleaned up" neighborhoods like Mountain View, they failed to address what made them dangerous in the first place.

I wondered if hard work, education, and good luck would push me out into the great suburban sprawl, push me into some safer, wealthier place where I would forget my time on Taku and watch with half-hearted concern as crime moved from one street to another without ever touching me in the deep, intimate way that forced me to acknowledge its reality.

❧

Deng Ba Dang was stumbling up the stairs, and I couldn't remember if I locked the door. I shot out of bed and ran toward it, slamming my full weight against the fiberglass material. Deng tried to enter. I managed to lock the bolt and the knob. He smashed against it with his shoulder, and I heard the wood of the doorframe splinter.

Adrenaline turns some people into action stars and others into Bambi. I was a deer-in-the-headlights type. My hand shook, and I couldn't remember how to use my fingers or dial 911. Concentrating mightily, I was finally able to connect with the emergency dispatcher.

Deng was yelling, "Open the door, Sarah!" I couldn't hear the operator clearly.

"I don't know why he's trying to get in," I said to the emergency dispatcher. Deng gave up on the door and started working on the window beside it.

"He's going to break my window!"

Before the glass shattered, he moved to the next door and began pounding.

"I think he's gone," I said. Another man began bashing my window and yelling Deng's name.

The dispatcher said the police would be there any minute and to lock myself in another room. The only "room" in the studio apartment was the bathroom and the door didn't latch, let alone lock. Nevertheless, I sat on the bathroom floor with my back against it and waited for the reassuring sound of sirens. The man stopped before the police arrived.

I stayed on the floor in the bathroom for a long time after the police came, smoking indoors, using my toilet as an ashtray. Later, Lou came to check on me. I learned that one of Deng's friends had tried to stab Deng in the neck. Deng caught the knife with his hand and ran from his apartment barefoot. When I didn't let him in, Deng went to Lou, who opened his door. The second man who'd pounded on my window was the one who had stabbed Deng and was hunting him down. The police caught and arrested Deng's stabber.

I slept late the next morning and didn't leave the apartment until after noon. The door was covered in blood. It dried on the handle and in rusty drops that led down the stairs and around the corner. Dark red handprints and smudges marked the doors of the neighbors who had turned Deng Ba Dang away.

⌒

When Deng lived next door, I complained several times to the landlord that he and his friends were harassing me. Some months before the stabbing incident, after one of his friends pounded on my door in the middle of the night, and eventually broke in because he "just wanted to talk," the landlord had offered Deng an apartment on the other side of the building, which at least moved him out of my path. He was finally evicted after two of his friends raped a teenage girl they had been partying with. Deng claimed he was sleeping when the sexual assault occurred. The victim escaped. She ran, naked from the waist down, and waited for the police in a stranger's home.

I saw Deng once, two years after I moved from Taku Drive. I had graduated and found a job with a nonprofit that offered great health insurance. For a little extra income, I taught on the weekends in the Hiland Mountain Correctional Center, Alaska's largest prison for women.

One Saturday in the visitor's lobby at Hiland, I recognized the back of Deng Ba Dang's shiny, bald head. He'd squeezed his large frame into a tiny, blue chair. As I turned my keys into the guards at the front desk, he recognized my voice.

"Sarah? What are you doing here?"

I didn't bother to correct him. "I teach here." And then, because I couldn't resist, "What are *you* doing here?"

"Visiting Lindy."

"Lindy?"

"Lindy Rae. Rae. She got in trouble," he said, and shook his head.

I didn't know Rae was serving time. I wouldn't have recognized her legal name on the roster. I said good-bye to Deng and drove home to Google the details.

Around six months after she had turned eighteen, Lindy Rae Morrison went to meet an acquaintance, Tyler Meyer, who owed her money. Tyler had been in rehab for months and was eager to buy crack from Rae, who had apparently been dealing. According to police records, Tyler met Rae and her driver in the middle of the night. Rae got out of the passenger seat and took Tyler's fifty dollars. She climbed back in the truck and handed Tyler an empty napkin she picked up from the floorboard, telling the driver to take off. Tyler grabbed the side of the truck, and the driver tried to shake him off by swerving the vehicle. The driver told police he didn't realize he had struck Tyler and dragged him for several blocks. Rae was found guilty of second-degree murder.

My initial thought was this: I hope she gets a long sentence, because she'll be safe in Hiland. Rae's dad, however, could afford a decent defense attorney. She was released after her sentencing, on time served.

❧

On the Thursday before Thanksgiving, a few dozen business executives will gather in the Anchorage Sheraton to launch the fundraising season. The hotel staff will dress sixty round tables, each just large enough to seat ten, in white linen overlays and crimson cloth napkins. Twenty plastic pines will hedge the ballroom, modestly wrapped in soft lights and topped with bows, not stars, not angels.

Servers will fill water glasses and place warm breadbaskets near the centerpieces right before the table hosts arrive. These executives will be friendly, but competitive; they will know one another from rotaries, galas, or the golf course. They may even sit on the same advisory boards. Alaska has more nonprofits per capita than anywhere else in the United States and the pool of generous advisors is miniscule. The social-services community, despite its great size, is strapped under the nation's highest rates of suicide, rape, and substance abuse. And so, every year men and women in pressed suits and soft blouses will gather here for brunch. The menu, the people, and the theme will alter only slightly.

I worked the Season of Giving charity luncheon for four years as part of a small development team. My last event was themed "Home for the Holidays." On the center of each table a handmade gingerbread house rested on a bed of cotton snow. I rushed from table to table, sprinkling the candied roofs with silver glitter.

Our team's goal was to raise $120,000 for the Salvation Army. For this to happen, each of the six hundred guests would need to donate at least $200 to one of the table hosts' kettles during the five-minute bell-ringing competition. This average was unlikely. Most of the guests would give just enough to cover the cost of the

39

meal, but fundraisers can count on the 80/20 rule: 80 percent of the donations come from 20 percent of the donors.

When the ballroom doors finally opened, I was covered in glitter and sweating profusely in an ill-fitting pinstripe suit. I walked against the crowd, heading for my position behind the scenes, when a familiar male voice asked, "Don't I know you?"

The voice belonged to Rae's dad, who I hadn't seen since our bitter argument over that $450 security deposit that the original landlord promised as a moving-in bonus. I was face-to-face with the man who had raised my rent twice but never bothered to replace my broken refrigerator. He crossed his arms over his chest when he recognized me and tilted up his chin. I was not supposed to be there. I should have been in those complexes across town, not mingling with these benefactors, whose money goes to reshuffling poverty and keeping it invisible. I offered to escort him to his seat, but he declined.

In the greeting area a string quartet played while the guests slipped off their scarves and gloves and wool jackets, a line of ushers ready to escort them to their seats. *If I stood near the rack with my arms open, would they drape their coats over me?* I wondered.

My former landlord's gift would put us $10,000 over our goal that day. When I reconciled the books for that event, I felt like I was counting Monopoly money—not the bright orange stacks of $500 notes, but the hard-earned small bills that come from the Baltic Avenues, that low-rent stretch of board that requires a community chest and leads directly to jail.

# OPEN HOLDS

I knocked Christopher off his feet when I opened my truck door. I might never have spoken with him at all if he hadn't been directly in my path. By then I knew that the smartest course of action on Taku was to mind my own business. I had pulled into the parking lot of my no-bedroom, 450-square-foot "apartment" and lingered an extra few minutes in the driver's seat to finish listening to a song, something maudlin and angsty, I'm sure. I didn't want to go inside at all because it was March, a month that straddles winter and spring and brings with it a general irritability after a long Alaska winter. I was just so tired of being inside. We had that in common.

"Hi, lady," the boy lying at my feet said. He held up a hand, a cue for me to help him up. Instead, I stared down at him while he pushed himself back to standing position. Normally, I wouldn't have remembered many details about a child's appearance—I wasn't a mom yet, and children all looked generically cute, like puppies or kittens or any newly formed creature, and they invoked mostly fear and annoyance, emotions that I had neither the patience nor willingness to understand. But that boy was as classically memorable as a Norman Rockwell subject: blond hair, blue eyes, and a plate-round face as symmetrical as a Disney character. He wore Oshkosh B'gosh overalls with a windbreaker. No winter coat. I thought *someone is missing him, someone close,* but easily dismissed the pang of worry.

I said something like, "Hi, kid. Watch out," and turned back to the truck's cab to gather my things. He stayed close as I headed toward my stairs, close the way children do, so unaware of personal space that if I'd stopped walking, he would have bumped into me. I ignored this. I didn't want his parents, whoever they were, to discover me talking with their child and get the wrong idea. I should say here too that I was single and self-concerned (which might be a redundancy), and I didn't want to draw any attention from my neighbors, who I, perhaps unfairly, assumed were all armed.

"Do you know where I live?" he asked, still following. "I can't remember, and Jaden's mom said he can't play outside and I can't come inside because he's being mean to his sister."

I scanned the windows facing my parking lot. There were no overprotective mothers watching us. In fact, most of the curtains in the vicinity were still closed.

"He's in there somewhere." He pointed to the nearest building, four stories of rental units with dozens of doors and windows.

"Is that where you live?"

"No. I live in a yellow house with a brown roof."

*So helpful*, I thought. He stared at me with curiousness. I was not used to the frank appraisal of children. His cheeks were dark pink from the cold that had not yet lost its February seriousness. I might have been a little squeamish about the snot streaming straight from his nose and into his mouth (something I wouldn't even see now), but his vulnerability was grossly conspicuous and even I couldn't look away.

⁓

I never wandered far in the winter. I stayed on my block, as near the woodstove and hot chocolate as a child could while still filling as many hours as possible with sled rides down snow piles. One spring day—very similar to the day I met Christopher—the sky was a Dodger blue dome, and both the sun and moon were visible. The beach was pulling me, and I was restless for the ocean and tide pools and hermit crabs. I wandered alone to the cruise ship dock in Haines, the small town where I was born. Only it wasn't a cruise ship dock yet and wouldn't be for twenty years. In 1987 it was just a long pier standing by the remnants of the town's first harbor, which was reduced to tarred and barnacled logs poking up at low tide. Normally, my second-oldest brother, Seth, would have been a chaperone, but he had left home an autumn earlier, *so sick of this town and its bullshit.* My mom, a single mother, was likely working or recovering from work as a bartender.

At the beach I gathered straw and seashells and really cool rocks. Century-old shipwrecks, with sand and ants spilling from their crevices, lined the shore. For me they were long-fallen giants, sleeping on their sides. I played at their feet, exploring and gathering, pretending to captain. I couldn't use the bathroom at the Quickstop unless I bought something, so when the urge came I looked for a private place. The wooden holds of the shipwrecked giants were split wide open by a half century or more of winter storms. There were no leaves on the trees yet, so the bushes wouldn't work for cover, and I *really* had to go.

I scanned the area for familiar houses. Did I have a friend nearby who would let me use her bathroom? The land sloped up from the ocean steeply, the Fort Seward part of town poised above the bay. Large Victorian structures lined the ridges, making Haines look like a quaint New England town from the air. In truth, Fort Seward was a military installation, meant to police rowdy miners during the gold rush. For me, the old white buildings looked so obviously haunted that I would avoid them no matter how much I had to use the restroom.

From the beach I could see the field where Seth taught me to fly a kite. He had taken me everywhere with him when he lived at home. When I could not keep up with him, he carried me, and when I grew too heavy to be carried, he found a solution. (The last time I visited Haines, someone I have no memory of said, *I remember when Seth used to pull you everywhere in a little red wagon.*) Seth would have known what to do, I thought. I needed something near. I spotted a nice house, gray with big beach-facing windows. Behind the glass an adult woman moved about. I don't know why I chose that house, why I thought it would be safe.

When she answered my knocking, I blurted, "Can I use your bathroom?" I think this made her laugh. It's hard to say. She may have regarded me with the same trepidation I gave Christopher, but in my memory she's morphed into a cheerful big-haired chubby

woman (who, now that I'm thinking about her, looked suspicious-
ly similar to Paula Deen). She smelled like cookies. She let me inside
and led me across plush carpets and spotless linoleum to a bathroom
near her kitchen.

On my way out, I could see Glacier Bay and the beach I'd combed.
The snow-covered mountains that normally seemed to loom over
town appeared pastoral and dreamy from where I was. I felt like I'd
made it inside a glass orb, inside something ideal.

"Did you wash your hands?" the woman asked me.

I hadn't. She ushered me over to her kitchen sink, turned on the
water, and asked my name. I asked her for a cookie. I ran the warm
water over my hands long after they were clean, not wanting to leave.

"I don't have any cookies," she said.

"Then what's that smell?"

"It's a cake."

"Can I have a piece?"

"It's for somebody's wedding. Have you ever seen a wedding
cake?" she asked.

"Only at my brother's wedding. It was strawberry cake with
vanilla frosting, and it was beautiful, but I like vanilla cake and
strawberry frosting."

"What's your brother's name, dear?"

"Which one?"

"The one who had the wedding cake."

She knew my brother Corkey, we discovered, and had in fact
baked the cake I described. I thought for sure she would give me a
piece of whatever smelled so good because she knew my oldest
brother, and *everybody* liked him, I was certain.

But she only said, "I see," alert to who my family was and why
I roamed around unsupervised, inviting myself into the home of a
stranger. She propped her hands on her hips, striking the classic
Superwoman pose.

"How old are you, Mary Beth?"

"Almost eight," I said, knowing the exact number of days left
until my birthday.

"I bet you should check in at home," she said. "It's getting close to dinnertime, and it sounds like you're hungry."

"I guess so." I dragged my feet all the way to the door.

I was almost back to the road when she called out to me, "When's your birthday?"

"June 13!" I said, and headed toward home.

☙

I didn't know what to do with the boy following me up the stairs. I couldn't drive him anywhere—what if someone thought I was abducting him? I could have called the police, but I didn't think they would arrive in a timely manner. I had called them recently for a woman who lived alone in the apartment behind mine. She was trapped inside while one of our other neighbors, drug violent and wanting her, kicked in her door. She slipped past him and hid in my apartment. The police came several hours later, long after her door had been broken open, as though they thought a woman ought to know better than to live alone in East Anchorage. The police inspected her splintered frame, the door that would no longer close or lock, and advised her to make a complaint to the landlord. The woman didn't insist they arrest the man, as though she too thought she ought to have known better.

I hoped the boy didn't wander as far from home as I did when I was a child. Haines was a small town, population just over a thousand at the time. The long distances trekked in my youth were likely shorter than my memory recalled. The boy lived in a rough part of Alaska's biggest city if he lived anywhere near me, and I assumed he did but thought to ask if his mom had dropped him off.

"No. But I wanted to play with Jaden, so I came to get him, but his mom says he's in trouble and he can't play. She's mean."

At the door of my apartment I said, "Wait right here. Okay? I'm going to walk you back home." He nodded. When I came back out, he was trying to slip his head between the bars of the balcony.

"Which way is home?" I asked. He disengaged from the railing and looked around.

"It's somewhere over there." He pointed south. There were small houses a few blocks into the neighborhood, an elementary school where the District 22 folks voted, and softball fields beyond that, but I didn't think he came that far on his own.

"Let's trace your way back, okay? What is your name?"

"Christopher."

"All right, Christopher, did you come down this hill?" I pointed to Fireoved, a street I suspected was misspelled and then renamed, which ended at my driveway where it intersected with another.

"Yes," he looked up at me. "Do you think I'm going to be in trouble?"

I thought of the sorts of trouble he could get into in our neighborhood. I (just barely) had the sense not to scare him with stories of vicious dogs and pedophiles and men with guns. I told him I didn't know. We walked up the first block of Fireoved, past apartments with blankets for curtains, past a car on flat tires, past an overfull dumpster.

When we got to the first intersection, I pointed to a house and asked, "Did you walk by here?"

"Yeah. That dog scared me." Christopher pointed to an American pit bull laying in a chicken-wire enclosure. The dog watched us walk by without lifting his head, his eyes following our feet disinterestedly. Christopher was nervous, though, and slipped his hand in mine. His hand felt warm and soft as summer sand. *He's so small*, I thought. My concern about being accused of kidnapping lessened some, and I held onto him. After a couple blocks the houses appeared tidier, more like homes and less like rentals, but Christopher kept walking.

"What is your mom doing, Christopher?" I asked to make chitchat.

"She was tired, so she told us to play outside," he said.

"You and who?"

"My little sister."

His *little* sister. "Where is she?"

"I dunno."

We walked for about fifteen minutes, straight through a handful of no-light intersections. Christopher didn't show signs of stopping.

"Are you sure you came this far?" I asked.

"Yeah. I remember that house," he said, pointing to a two-story. "Guess how old I am."

"Eight." I estimated up, hoping to flatter him.

"No!" He said and laughed. He held up his one hand and one thumb. "I'm this many."

"Five?"

"Six!'

"Wow. Are you going to start school soon?" I asked.

"Yeah, I already did."

I told Christopher that I was in school too.

"No way!" he said. "You're way too *old* to be in school."

"I'm only twenty-seven," I said, my feelings a little hurt.

"Wow. You're *really* old. You're even older than my mom! She was in school, but she had to quit."

"Are we getting close?" We were almost to the elementary school. I heard children playing on the next block.

"Look, it's Tommy!" Christopher yelled, pointing with his whole arm to a boy in the distance. "My house is bigger than his!" He began pulling away, his feet itching to run to the other boys.

"Wait a second," I held his arm. "I need to talk to your mom. Where do you live?" He pointed to a yellowish duplex with a brown roof and leaned away from me, but I didn't let go. "Which door?"

A silver truck pulled out of the driveway Christopher had pointed to. I held onto his arm as he tried to wriggle out of my grip. The truck was coming toward us. It stopped in front of us, and the driver's side window rolled down. I let go of Christopher's arm and thought, *I'm going to get my ass kicked now*. But Christopher froze at the sight of the male driver, and I wanted, suddenly, to put myself between him and the man.

"Where's your sister?" the man asked. Christopher said he didn't know. And just like that, the man drove on. He barely looked at me. I asked Christopher if that was his dad.

"That's my sister's dad. Can I go play with Tommy now?"

"Go for it. I'm going to tell your mom you're with Tommy. Okay?"

"K. Byeeee," he said, stretching the last word into two syllables and already running.

I approached the door where I thought Christopher's mom might be and knocked. When no one answered, I knocked harder. As I turned away, the door opened and a woman around my age looked at me with sleep-crusted eyes. The house behind her was dark. She wore pajama bottoms, and her blonde hair hung in long tangles over a faded T-shirt.

"Hi," I said, hoping I didn't look like a crazy or a missionary. "I live by the highway, on Fireoved and Taku. Christopher walked all the way over there. By himself. I brought him home."

"Thanks," she said and shut the door. Firmly.

એ

The night before my eighth birthday, a special cake arrived at the American Legion where my mom worked. She didn't ask why I was gifted that cake or how I met the cake maker. Perhaps she already knew. The cake was suited for a princess, tiered like wedding confection, strawberry frosting over rich chocolate and a secret vanilla heart. But as delicious and pretty as it was, I felt anxious when my mom brought it home, embarrassed that it was delivered to a bar, embarrassed that I'd shown that woman how lonely I was. I don't know if it was that day or sometime soon after that I took to hiding in the gutted hold of my favorite wreck, where even on hot afternoons the sand inside stayed cool and damp. I wasn't afraid of the beetles or the sandworms that sheltered there. I wanted my brothers to come looking for me, but they had moved on. That summer I carried the sounds of waves and the smells of tar and seawater and rotting boards.

When I walked home from Christopher's, the silver truck passed me twice. The man, at least, was looking for his daughter. I was angry because I thought I knew something of the longing that pulled that boy so far away from his front yard. I assured myself that he had good instincts. He was the kind of kid who would find resources, regardless of how far it took him, and therein lay the tightrope of success and tragedy. Because I can't ever forget him, I let my hope for Christopher swell in me like a cake rising.

# PART TWO

# A MAN OF FASHION

Mark Coon makes a lot of noise when he moves, and he moves slowly. At my desk in the administrative offices of the Salvation Army, I close my eyes and listen for the bump-bump of his carved-bone cane and the whoosh of his leather—noises that precede him like the clinking of his chains and buttons and pins. Faded badges, sewn into his jacket long ago, exhibit his former bike chapters. His newer badges display the number of years he has been in recovery. Mark has three sobriety badges, each for two years clean.

The sight of Mark leaning against the doorway makes me grin. In a religious nonprofit environment, he stands out like the clichéd black sheep—only picture a white sheep in worn leather. And cussing. And smoking. The office fills with the smell of Brute cologne and cigarettes.

"How you doing, Mark?"

"Well, I woke up sucking air. So that's good. But these stairs are a bitch." He sounds winded. "Ever heard of an elevator?" He asks this nearly every day he comes. It's our routine. He acts older than he is, but years of hard living make this act believable. He has the face of a man who spent decades working physically, playing hard, and riding without a helmet—tattoos, gold chain, scars on scars. At forty-eight, he already has a pacemaker.

"What do you have for me today?" he asks as he moves to the volunteer workstation. He tucks his cane under the desk and pulls Ding Dongs and Dr. Pepper from a plastic grocery bag.

"A whole lot of the same thing," I say.

"Good. I'll try to be of use. Where's Cool Breeze?" Cool Breeze is his nickname for the development director, Josie, a woman who walks and talks fast and always at the same time. Mark frequently says of her, "The only way I know she's been in the room is by the cool breeze on my neck."

*Dress for the job you want, not the job you have*, Josie's given to reciting like a mantra.

"I got a new shirt she's going to like," he says, slipping his leather jacket off his shoulders. Although he is a volunteer, Josie has been encouraging him to dress up more. Last month we had a big fundraiser to kick off the holiday season. The event was a luncheon, and the dress was recommended as business "executive." To avoid hurting Mark's pride, I intercepted Josie's enthusiastic advice as much as possible, but she had called Mark into her office ahead of time and given him a fifty-dollar gift card to get something "professional."

The morning of the event I found Mark outside of the ballroom of the Sheraton Hotel tucking his shirt in his pants. The gift card was enough for him to rent the top half of a tuxedo, which he wore over jeans with cowboy boots and his big, black Stetson.

"Do I look okay?" he had asked, uncharacteristically self-conscious.

"Texas charming, my friend."

But he didn't go over the top today. I see a new pale-blue, button-up shirt under a layer of flannel, tucked into his soft, gray jeans. He mostly wears old tennis shoes, but today he wore his cowboy hat, which means he walked here on heeled boots. "You always wear boots with a Stetson," he told me once. "Texas rule."

If you ask Mark about his nickname, he'll say, "They call me Hard Walkin' because I make walking look hard. I'm always walking—the court won't ever give me back my license." For long journeys, he relies on Anchor Rides, a public transit service for the handicapped. With five felony DUIs under his enormous belt buckle, it is unlikely he will ever drive legally again. Every couple of years he falls off the wagon and starts over this familiar cycle of recovery—drink for a time with no consequence, drive illegally, go to jail, get sober.

When I first started working at "Sally's," as Mark calls it, I was told that the phrase "on the wagon" was coined by men and women receiving social services in the late nineteenth century. Evangeline Booth, daughter of the founder, drove her hay wagon through the streets of New York. She called to the inebriates in the street, the impoverished: *Climb on board for a ride back to the Salvation Army's soup kitchens for healing and gospel.* This would have been during America's great temperance movement, which would eventually lead to the prohibition of alcohol. Whole countries make their way on and off that wagon, one citizen at a time.

Mark's temperance movement began early in 1998, while spending his last day in the Spenard Motel, just four blocks away from his favorite bar, the Carousel. A storm had shouldered its way to the edge of the city, and the air pushing through the window seeped with cold humidity. Mark sat on the double bed where pale light of the late afternoon exposed cigarette burns and food stains on the blankets. He doesn't remember exactly how the room looked, just that it smelled nasty and you couldn't walk barefoot on the carpet. It was used mostly by prostitutes and by partiers like him.

Mark had spent the last of his money buying an eighteen-pack of Budweiser and renting the movie *Leaving Las Vegas.* All he had in the world was in that room, minus the five-dollar key deposit, and he would need to give the front desk more cash if he wanted to stay through the night. He'd blown through an inheritance and several decent jobs just trying to stay drunk. He was still recovering from a severe motorcycle accident a few months before. At five feet and eleven inches tall, Mark had partied himself down to 113 pounds and had few teeth left.

"I thought I looked damn good back then," Mark told me once, "the cat's meow. I remember looking at myself in the mirror the day before I wrecked my bike, thinking, 'Damn, I'm gonna get laid tonight.'" But when he finished watching Nicolas Cage's character drink himself to death, he saw himself as if for the first time and threw his beer away. He called his mom to borrow money.

"I knew she didn't trust me," he says, "because I wasn't trust-worthy. I asked her to rent me a room, and then she gave me the single best thing she ever gave me—apart from my existence—and I love her for that."

On January 3, 1998, just as the sky opened its big, white arms to blanket Anchorage in a foot of snow, Mark's mother finally, finally said no.

And now, thirteen years later, Mark is scheduled to graduate from a last-ditch treatment program, which means that he won't be coming to Sally's as much. In January 2010, the Anchorage Wellness Court required Mark to provide twelve hours of community service a week to a nonprofit organization. This was bullshit, he thought. After years of pushing the proverbial stone up bureaucracy hill, undergoing back surgery and brain surgery, and blowing both knees, he was finally declared fully disabled by the Veteran's Administration. He shouldn't have to volunteer. But this was phase two of the program, the "go to court once a month, piss in a cup" phase, as he described it to me the first day we met. "They want to keep us bastards busy—idle hands and all that."

"I'm going to jump through hoops until I graduate," he said. "They want me to 'volunteer,' I'll volunteer. If they want me to turn my head and cough, I'll turn my head and cough. But I'm not going to prison."

A little background—Alaska parties like it's 1999. We spend many months in the dark, followed by the briefest summer of manic, twenty-four-hour light. In an effort to conform to our environment, our internal landscapes begin to match the extremities of our climate. Alaska's high alcohol and drug abuse rates go hand in hand with increased DWI arrests, suicides, domestic and sexual violence—the Molotov cocktail of a city self-medicating. It is a part of our culture and perhaps one of the reasons Mark and I share an ease in each other's company. We know this landscape. We are both what psychologists call ACOAs—adult children of alcoholics, though both of our mothers had quit drinking many years earlier.

The idea behind the Anchorage Wellness Court falls under the blanket term of *therapeutic jurisprudence*, and it saves many families from losing a loved one to the prison system. The goal of the court is to decrease recidivism among offenders by addressing the more complex issues leading to the criminal behavior. Instead of going to prison for drunk driving after his fifth felony DWI, Mark opted for the eighteen-month treatment program that would require abstinence from alcohol, group therapy, individual therapy, community service, and frequent court attendance.

The Salvation Army considered Mark a community work service volunteer. Free labor. Normally, he would have been given a physical task in a thrift-store warehouse, but poor health made him harder to place. In one of his sober periods, he had done some data entry for the Veterans Administration, so I paired up with Mark because I needed assistance keeping up with data cleanup and miscellaneous tasks. There is never enough staff in the nonprofit world. That's a fact. Sally's feared adequate staffing would lead to shameful administrative costs.

When the court ordered Mark to volunteer, he didn't want to be here, mainly because he doesn't like being told what to do. "I am a disabled vet," he said. "*Fully* disabled." But now he says he looks forward to coming in.

"So are you going to clean your desk out today?" I ask. Mark uses a desk between me and the administrative assistant. It displays a picture of him on a motorcycle, another picture of himself fishing with Jim Belushi (a privilege he won from a call-in radio contest), and a toy raccoon imprisoned by a miniature cage. "I'll let him out on Graduation Day," Mark has told me several times. Graduation day will be whenever he next phases up and out of Wellness Court. Soon.

"I think they're going to keep me in a little longer," he says. Unfortunately, he keeps butting heads with the wrong people and is spending longer than normal in phase two. He nicknamed his parole officer "Special K." He gives most people nicknames. I don't always understand the rationale behind them.

"Special K gave me an *assignment*," he says, emphasizing the word. I can tell by the tone of his voice that he didn't take it seriously. When he talks about his interactions with Special K, I'm reminded of the boy in high school who always ended up in the hall for sassing. The assignment this time was a "recovery collage." When men and women in the program are out of line, they are told to submit an extra urine analysis or write essays answering questions like, "How do you prioritize treatment, school, and recovery meetings?" The recovery collage was part of Mark's Moral Reconation Therapy, a cognitive-behavioral treatment approach designed to strengthen his moral reasoning. Perhaps Special K thought a collage would be right up his alley, as he was, in sober periods, an award-winning artist.

"Let me ask you something, Ms. Mary." He reaches into the inner pocket of his leather jacket and pulls out a folded piece of paper. He makes his way out of his chair and wobbles over to my desk with his assignment. "Does this seem inappropriate to you?"

Mark often asks about appropriateness, as I did when I began work at the Salvation Army. He hands me his drawing. It's a big circle cut into pie pieces, each slice with a sketch to represent a cycle of the recovery program. There is a cross in one, a hand reaching out in another. One picture is of a penis with a trail of urine splashing into a plastic cup.

"Yeah. Special K might find that inappropriate," I say. "Good picture though. Real nice collage."

"Thank you," he says, pleased with himself.

᎗

Today is Mark's graduation, and I'm getting ready for court in the bathroom at work, waiting for the curling iron to heat up and applying the expensive makeup my mother had bought me at Nordstrom the day before my wedding. I will have to get more soon and dread the thought of going to a mall. The bathroom, like the rest of the building, has a kept-up façade. Our fiscally conservative boss is trying to get just a few more years out of it. The divisional headquarters, like the rest of Sally's, is fighting to stay current, to become something more than your grandmother's charity.

The dim yellow light sinks into dull, beige tiles. Former staff attempted to brighten up the bathroom with plastic plants and kitsch artwork of framed text—the "Live, Laugh, Love" variety. I'm spending time on my appearance for court at Josie's request. Normally, I don't wear a lot of makeup or hair product to work. I spend the majority of my time behind a computer unless we have a fundraiser or media event.

"You look good for events, Mary. You should really look that good every day," Josie had suggested. I'm trying to forget the rest of that conversation as I begin to curl my hair, but I can't help but replay it: "Sometimes I want to send you to events in the community, but I take one look at you—and I don't."

My face reddens as I recall Josie's statement, and I see the beginning of a wrinkle in my brow. I have a face that looks angry or happy, not much in between, so I consciously have to remind myself to smile in public. After I finish my makeup, I clip my hair into a horn at my forehead so I can curl the bottom layer. Even in my best gray suit and softest purple blouse, I still see myself as rough around the edges, low class. Poor. There are so many days that I want to quit trying to fit into this culture, quit jumping through the hoops.

Although what Josie said was cruel, I recognize that she said it under the banner of good intentions; she is a friend, and she knows that I put myself through college waitressing and didn't know how to dress any better than Mark when I left home. But I took her comments personally and have been irritated by them for weeks. On days when Mark senses that I'm not fitting into the mold, he tells me to keep my chin up. When class-passing, you no longer belong where you came from or fit in where you are. It's an essential loneliness. I wonder if Mark feels as isolated as I do at times, with his old friends still drinking and himself not yet sure how to socialize in the sober world.

My hair is now in the throwback '50s bob of which I know Josie approves. I lift my chin and catch the eyes of the divisional commander's wife as she comes into the bathroom. At Sally's, husband and wife ministers get promoted together and are given the same rank, although they have separate roles that fit traditional gender lines. Husband and Wife Major are the highest-ranking officers in the Alaska Division; they also happen to be fourth- and fifth-generation ministers who I doubt have ever seen the inside of a bar.

"You look so pretty," Wife Major says. "Have you been losing weight?"

I tell her it's a slenderizing outfit, but the compliment is well timed; my self-esteem is fish-tailing, and I need to present a confident persona.

"I noticed it the other day. I was going to say something about how good you look, but there were men around," she says. It takes me a minute to understand what she's talking about, a testament to the different universes we come from. *Is it really improper to bring attention to a woman's appearance in front of a man?* I think.

As she leaves—her tidy skirted uniform looking perfectly decent—I remember one of the first conversations I had with her. She said she always carbon copies Husband Major whenever she has occasion to email a man, just to be transparent. Giggling, I try to imagine what my husband, Peter, would think of that. Would he find it absurd? Would it make him suspicious? I put my makeup away and run the rod of the curling iron under cold water before putting it in my bag.

With my face stretched into a smile, I spread glitter-pink Dior gloss slowly across my lips. There are so many moments in my past, public and private, that would curl the majors' hair. I am *of* the world, fully. Sinful, ornery, and proud.

Salvationists do not drink. It would be hypocritical, it was explained to me, with the Salvation Army responsible for so many recovery programs. I go to a Lutheran church. My pastor will occasionally drink beer and eat bratwurst. He said in a recent sermon, "Jesus drank with the sinners and went amongst them."

When I imagine Jesus as he may have been twenty centuries ago, drinking with new friends, I can't imagine that he glided, ethereal, into some inn and projected a sanctimonious persona. By accounts, Jesus was a man of humility and compassion, without airs. I also speculate—and I hope that's allowed—at His many unknown and undocumented acts of kindness and humility, executed quietly and without ado.

I think of Mark's graduation with a little sadness, knowing I won't see him as often. No matter where I came from, or how humble my position, Mark will never look at me sideways. Another reason I'm worried about Mark's graduation is that it implies he is recovered. We like to fix problems and be done with it. That's the problem with addiction—there is no safe distance; it's never over.

On weekends I teach in a correctional center for women. Most of the ladies are inside for crimes either directly or indirectly related to drugs or alcohol. A woman is sober inside because she has to be. She may be determined to stay that way, to change her life, but within months, sometimes weeks after her release, she will be back in prison and back to square one. It's the revolving door. It is the same people, the same problems, over and over and over again.

It's almost impossible, even for the most fervent advocate of social change, not to get disheartened by this. Terms like *burnout* and *compassion fatigue* describe what occurs to many clergy, mental health professionals, emergency care workers, human service workers, and volunteers. Often, people who start out caring the most become disillusioned. A symptom of compassion fatigue is increased cynicism and dehumanized perceptions of people; the caregiver begins labeling clients in a derogatory manner. The former idealist transforms into a cynic.

I put my stuff away and run downstairs before Husband Major beats me to the kitchen. I'm just in time to see him add a single scoop of Folgers to the old grinds, which he stretches into ten cups of brown water. His family has been in the salvation business for many generations; he prides his penny-pinching genes and lives in an impoverished state with a certain amount of smugness. Sally's prides itself on its care ethics. Only eight cents on the dollar is used for administrative costs, according to internal reports. Of course, the pay structure for officers is such that the organization meets all of their basic needs—housing, transportation, uniforms, and a stipend—so although they live modestly, they live without the same risks of the real poor, who have to ask questions like, "Should I pay rent on time or buy groceries?"

Since Mark arrived, my office has been increasingly productive. It's almost like being fully staffed. I boast about him a little to Husband Major while we wait for the coffee to brew. High productivity and free labor are sure to please him.

"You say he's in Wellness Court?" he asks.

"Yes, sir. And he's going to graduate today," I say, with a little pride.

"These people—you have to be careful. Keep your boundaries. They are in and out of our programs all the time." He leaves me in the kitchen, percolating.

Anchorage is divided into many camps when it comes to dealing with its chronic inebriate homeless population, and I know that is what is shaping the major's fatalism about alcoholics. It has been a hot-button issue in the local press: what do we treat first, the alcoholism or its symptom, homelessness?

"Just because they are drunks doesn't mean they deserve to live like that," argue those in favor of treating the symptom first.

Anchorage has a mayor-appointed committee tasked with addressing the issue. In 2009 and 2010, deaths among street people rose dramatically. On the corners of busy intersections, men and women hold signs that say things like, "NO LIES I JUST NEED A BEER." Nearly every morning on my way to Sally's, I drive by the same man on the corner of Northern Lights and C Street. His sign says, "Sober 16 years. Will work for food." Like many Anchoragites, I don't want to give him money because I think he will use it for booze. I think he's a liar. If the light is red, I try to give him something from my lunch. I'd like to think it's altruism that makes me lean across the passenger seat and dangle a banana or a granola bar out of the window. I usually feel really good about myself for a few blocks.

I know that it is the guilt as much as the good in me that makes me share. The guilt at those brown eyes that look into me over the cardboard, eyes that see I have been lucky. I can afford to give more and I don't. I could look at him, actually look at him, and see the horrid reality of how he must live, but when it's twenty-one degrees below zero and I am under a soft blanket, snuggled up to the clean, warm body of my husband, I think only of what is mine.

When I asked Mark how long he was homeless after his mom refused to get him a room, he said, "Not too long. I walked all the way to the east side in the snow, trying to get to Tudor Rescue Mission. They preach a little God, but the food is good. I collapsed right across the street and the rescue workers took care of me."

"Were you ever like the men that hold the signs?" I asked.

"No. I never held a sign. But I did tell the bartender at the Carousel that my mom died so I could get free drinks."

Mark once told me he saw a street man walk behind a dumpster and throw fruit on the ground, bananas, oranges, apples—the same food people hold out their car windows.

Mark said, "That's why I don't give them anything except for money sometimes. When they're honest."

⁓

"January 13, 2011. 2:00 p.m." The court clerk says this into the recorder.

"Judge!" A man in Carhartts and a T-shirt shouts from the back of the courtroom, as soon as Judge Swiderski is seated. "Can I go first? I have to be at work by three o'clock."

I sit three rows back in the center of Wellness Court, which looks and sounds like a loosely controlled classroom. Men and women in various states of casual dress loudly heckle each other. Judge Swiderski, a white-haired man with steady eyes and a slow manner of speaking, takes the call-and-response casualness in stride.

Mark has been in the program twenty-three months, about six months longer than most, on account of his hard-headedness. When it is finally his turn, Mark stands before the judge doing his best impression of the Man in Black—legs apart, shoulders back, Stetson off, and hands clasped by his biggest buckle.

"Okay, Mark Coon. Let's do it," Judge Swiderski starts. "You have the right to say something before I impose judgment."

"Impose away, your Honor," Mark says, all business. All Texas.

"Three years suspended. Two years of probation. Your license is permanently revoked. Forfeit registration of any vehicle you own. Oh, that's right—we need to get your mother on the phone."

"It's her birthday today," Mark says. A blush moves up his neck as he looks down.

"What a great present," says the judge.

The voice of Mark's mother comes over the speakers. She sounds like the cookie-cutter version of any mom or grandma, sweet and a little shaky, a voice that could comfort or condemn. The judge explains to her that the court is invited to speak about Mark, of experiences with him, for or against him.

One by one people around me stand and share stories of a subversive man, a man who didn't take recovery seriously when he began, and a man who submitted and transformed himself. "I'm so proud of you, Mark," was the most repeated expression. "Proud that you learned to surrender."

*Mark? Surrender?* I thought. *Never.*

This idea of surrender is paramount in the language of recovery. Mark struggles with this concept the most. Today, when a man says he is sober, the statement has a lot of connotations. A man who is sober has already blown his doors open, has possibly spent a period of his life as sober's antonym, maybe woke in his own vomit, in a strange bed, in the wrong city. There is a culture of recovery in America complete with its own assumptions, literature, medicine, religion, and communities. I'm getting a peek inside. As I watch each member of Wellness Court stand up to beam, it is clear that Mark is a venerable member of this group. In this community he is a popular gentleman. A socialite.

Someone from our agency should say something, in support of both Mark and Wellness Court. I manage, red-faced and unprepared, to stammer out how proud I am. To the court and Mark's peers, I'm the face of Sally's, supporting Mark's tentative first steps into the sober world and their own. He did good.

Judge Morris, another Wellness Court judge, has come down

from his chambers to see Mark graduate. He speaks last. This large, ruddy-faced bear of a man worked with Mark several times in the past.

"It's good to see you," he starts. "Good for many reasons. Good because there were times I never expected you to make it. There was just so much stacked against you. I suppose that's the point about the bullheadedness and surrendering," he says, referencing the earlier speeches.

"You had to deal with more pain, more physical pain and real barriers, than anyone who has been through this court, and you had to be incredibly strong to deal with the bureaucracy that gets in your way—the Veteran's Administration, hospitals, even public transit."

Judge Morris pauses before continuing. Mark's face is a beet.

"You had to balance the need to be really strong to get over those objective problems, but your success was delayed by your bullheadedness when it came to addiction." Judge Morris looks out at the court because his next words are for all of us.

"You figured out how to walk a balanced life, to stay strong to get well, and then get out of the way of your own success."

I try to imagine Mark living a balanced life. I see myself on a similar teeter-totter, trying not to sink too far into the dangerous past or put too much hope into the unknown future.

A woman who teaches Buddhist meditation to prison inmates told me once about a concept called the Middle Way, a path of moderation that exists between sensual indulgence and self-denial. I can see Mark's conundrum in the picture Judge Morris has painted. Here is a man whose strength is stubbornness. It is what allowed him to quit drinking in the first place, and he doesn't want to lose it to the court, or to the serenity-prayer-chanting twelve-step community that constantly calls for his complete abdication.

Judge Morris continues. "You look good, Mark. So much better than you did at times in the program when we could see you were in pain. You were strung out and having a hard time, not just from the pain, but the struggles with addiction."

"Ms. Coon?" he calls up toward the speakers. "When was the last time you saw Mark?"

"Oh, I don't know. At least five years," she says in her lilting, little-old-lady voice.

"So you really haven't seen him then. Well, he's seven foot two now, looks like a linebacker with hair down to his knees. He looks fat and sassy." He turns back to Mark with a twinkle in his eye and says, "Now you've shown us you're a man of fashion." At this the court laughs.

"You've got a coat and tie, hat, spiffy walking stick—I don't mean to be joking about that—it's an exhibition of your self-pride and self-esteem, your recognition that you won the battles you had to fight."

As Judge Morris wraps up his speech to Mark, I mull over the compliment he gave Mark's attire, thinking of Josie fussing about Mark's clothes and mine as well. Something about being here makes me want to try a little harder, to reconsider a value I judged as superficial and unimportant. Maybe in all our unconscious actions we show the world the battles that we fight, not just in our attire, but in our scars, mannerisms, speech, right down to the quality of our skin—and they signal to the world the nature of our struggle and the score.

After Judge Morris wraps up, Judge Swiderski looks at Mark. The speeches of the court brought Mark close to tears, and he puffs his chest up a bit.

"Do you have anything to say?" Judge Swiderski asks him. Over the loudspeaker Mark's mom interrupts.

"Yes, I do."

Judge Swiderski raises his eyebrows and smiles at Mark. "Go ahead, ma'am."

"I am so proud of you, Marky," she says, "and I had faith. I knew you could make it. I am so proud of you and so is your sister Kelly. I've never had a better birthday present."

"Your firstborn is going to be okay," Mark says for all of us to hear. "I love you, Mom."

"I know you are, honey. I love you too."

Early in March 2011, Mark drops by the office to set his raccoon free and "shoot the shit." Spring is right around the corner, bright and promising. Mark hobbles into the office noisily and in good cheer. I'm winter weary; a lifelong Alaskan learns to be ready for that last storm, the one that comes after weeks of melting snow piles and ceaseless blue skies.

He strikes up a conversation with the new volunteer I'm training to take his place. It's easy for Mark to make friends. He's not shy. Nate, a tall and wiry young man with a full sleeve of tattoos, is here as part of a work rehabilitation program that pays him to volunteer at Sally's. In return we help transition him back into full-time hours after a debilitating on-the-job injury.

After the two of them discuss a motorcycle-related mechanical issue that sounds to me like a foreign language, Nate says, "It's so cool to meet someone else who's into bikes, man. I don't have people I can talk to about this stuff."

"You sober?" Mark asks.

"Yes, sir," says Nate.

"I go to a bike club, Second to None. It's a bunch of old guys who like to ride, but they don't drink or do drugs. Call me sometime if you want to go." Mark pulls a card out of his pocket and hands it to Nate. The card has an emblem of a hand with a flame on the palm and says "Hard Walkin' Mark. Call before you use."

Mark has brought in a copy of a newspaper article to show me. It's from 2000 when he was profiled in the *Anchorage Daily News* as a "Face of Sobriety." The whole front page of the Life section shows a smiling Mark as he appeared a decade ago, hair and all. He looks similar, but thinner, his hair a long, brown mullet. The writer described his rough-and-tumble rap sheet as "long and mean."

"Wish I never did that interview," he tells me. "I fell off the wagon like three months after that. It's been a long journey getting clean. Over ten years."

I've heard that an alcoholic is emotionally frozen at the age they started drinking. As if to offer proof of this, Mark tells me that a few weeks back he had to be flown to Seattle for a staph infection in his knee. They sent him home with a strict regimen of antibiotics, including an IV bag. Mark had marched straight to his nearest tattoo parlor.

"Was that a good idea?" I ask.

"Well, I figured it's as good a time as any. I'm on all these antibiotics now."

A part of me expects Mark to fail again, that same part of me that doesn't trust a sunny March. Not because he's weak-willed, but because he's still learning how to be sober, how to have a long game. But the man I've come to know doesn't surrender. Not that easy. He drove illegally to his own graduation. I imagine that the unreachable dreams that plague him—getting his license back, walking without pain, being young and strapping—are only as vivid as the dream of being able to drink and do drugs again without it ruining his life.

Saying that I expect Mark to fail is how I protect myself from disappointment. I also know that if Mark relapses, he will try again, and again, and again to straighten himself out.

"What do you think, Mark? Is it going to snow again?" I ask. Mark is packing all his stuff up into a plastic grocery bag and getting ready to leave.

"I don't know," he says. He turns toward me, holding his raccoon in one hand, a miniature cage in the other. "I sure as hell hope not. Tell you what, though, I'm ready for summer, ready to ride."

Mark can't physically take his bike on the road anymore—never mind that he doesn't have a license—his knees aren't strong enough. But he can't bear to get rid of it. In the summer months, he parks his motorcycle in his front yard, lets the sun heat up the chrome and the black leather seats, and when he goes outside to smoke, he slips onto it. He rode for so long that the movement became muscle memory. It doesn't hurt too much to mount, to grip the throttle, to remember.

# THE REAL WOMEN OF
# HILAND MOUNTAIN

I stood between two bulletproof doors, waiting for one to close and the other to open. Fluorescent light hummed in the small space where guards and visitors left muddy boot prints on the white linoleum. People spend only seconds at a time between those doors—no more than the length of a few short breaths. I moved to the window so the guards could get a clear look at me. The door still didn't open.

A male voice crackled over the intercom. "I'm sorry—who did you say you were here with?"

"Education," I said. I'd been coming to the Hiland Mountain Correctional Center every Saturday and Wednesday for two years, but most of the guards didn't know my name or my face. They rotated their shifts weekly and their duties daily. So much to remember. So many women.

On the other side of the second door, a disembodied arm pushed my keys and a badge through a hole in the one-way-mirrored counter. Someone I never saw sat behind that glass to make sure only one door opened at a time and that all of the keys were accounted for. A low buzz from a wall speaker cleared me to push open a third reinforced door.

The song of stringed instruments wafted along the corridor as the inmate orchestra practiced in the cafeteria. To my left, locked Dutch doors secured the nurse's station. Before dinner, a line of sixty or seventy women would border the hallway as they sought their daily medication, but right then it was blessedly empty. I once thought dead-eyed, hard-hearted people went to prison to rape and make shanks of razors and sporks. Maybe they did on late-night cable. The first time I'd walked the hall, it felt like walking a plank: a hundred angry pirate eyes bored into me.

My boss, who had walked beside me that day, said, "Stare them right in the eye and call them by their last name. You'll learn their names soon enough. Good to see you, Smith." She had smiled at an inmate. The inmates looked away from her as she demonstrated. "Don't be intimidated."

I let the memory fade out and continued down the corridor. A passageway dipped to the left where another set of reinforced doors enclosed the Solitary Treatment Unit. I would visit a student there later, but at the moment I kept moving, past the little library, its meager shelves lined with donated genre fiction, past the law room, where inmates had access to legal books to help support their cases.

I'd found the Hiland job on Craigslist around the time that I lost my last serving job. I was never a good waitress—I'd once dropped a tray full of drink refills on a paraplegic man. Nor was food service good to me. The incident that stands out most in my memory was a surreal meeting with the floor manager at a hip breakfast café in downtown Anchorage.

The café was extremely popular, a favorite place for twenty-somethings to drink mimosas on Sunday morning. It was common for the wait time to reach an hour on the weekends. The servers were sassy and educated, pierced and tattooed. They seemed to know just where to stylishly rip their uniforms and just when to talk back to a grumpy customer. I never quite fit in. My sassy sounded rude, and my stylishly ripped looked frumpy. The manager was a bald, middle-aged woman who lived in her Volkswagen van. In the spring of 2008, she had asked me to come into the office and take a seat. I had suspected she was going to ask me if I was doing okay. She knew my brother Seth had committed suicide a few weeks before, that I was grieving and having a difficult time remembering details. I was leaving the dining room often for cigarette breaks. Perhaps too often.

"Mary, I'm concerned for our customers," the manager said. "You don't seem to hit your *groove* until nine in the morning. But we need you to be 'on' as soon as the doors open at seven."

What does that mean? I had asked. Please be specific, I said.

"You are not smiling enough between the hours of 7:00 and 9:00 a.m.," she specified.

I told her I would try to smile more in the mornings, but I checked out that day, determined to make that my last serving job. Throughout college, I'd kept a second, part-time job tutoring English at the university; that and my recently earned bachelor's qualified me to teach in Hiland.

The light surprised me when I'd first started working inside. When a non-felon imagines prison, light and flowers and music do not come to mind, but the entire right side of the hallway was lined with floor-to-ceiling windows through which I could see that it was visiting hour. Outside, women in yellow scrubs sat with their husbands, daughters, and fathers. Holding a Tonka truck out like a sword, a young boy ran through the flowerbeds verdant with purple and orange and green. Where the well-groomed courtyard wasn't surrounded by squat wood buildings, it was closed in by tall chain-link fences, rimmed with razor wire.

I reached the cafeteria, full of violins, cellos, and violas working in harmony to bring Beethoven back to life. Song filled the institution with tension and texture. *We have fallen into a place where everything is music,* Rumi said eight hundred years ago. He would have liked the scene before me: playing in chairs and leaning against tables, some of the hardest women in Alaska surrendered to their instruments. But not Diana Waggy. She sat at a table to the side, listening. Her eyes stared past the women and into the music itself.

Diana had stopped wrapping her head in a scarf. Her hair had grown back a different color, soft like a baby's, short, and brownish red. She looked younger than she had the week before, having survived the chemotherapy and radiation for breast cancer. She looked her age again, around fifty, her skin slowly ungraying, filling again with pink life.

"You made it," she said.

୶

Because my early impressions of prison were based on HBO dramas, I imagined they were all Alcatraz-style cement fortresses. Throw in some rampant homosexuality, corrupted guards, iron bars, chairs with straps, and so forth.

I thought that when a woman went to prison, her life was over, or at least her influence was, apart from the ripple effects of her crime. These ideas were reinforced when I was hired. I was shuffled to the administrative wing on my first day, the only section of the main building not wrapped in wire. The sergeant, a short barrel-shaped man nearing retirement age, was responsible for orienting the new teachers. He led me silently through a labyrinth of doors, not once looking back.

I followed the sergeant into a small conference room, where the only thing inside was an enormous, blond conference table with chairs. I sat in the seat nearest the door and breathed in stale air, waiting for him to say something. The walls weren't close but the ceiling was low; everything about the environment felt too big or too small, the scene both too bright and too dark with the buzzing rows of lights and the old, dirty carpet.

The sergeant had a way of creating awkward silence and then barking into it—I would learn later that many of the guards were versed with this skill. "You worked in a prison before!"

"No, sir," I said. The sergeant stood at the other side of the table looking down at me for a long time without breaking eye contact, his lips pressed so tightly together they appeared white. I began to remember every law I ever broke, every speeding sign I disregarded, times I may have had several drinks too many and drove home anyway. I was certain he knew I started smoking my mom's cigarettes long before I was nineteen, that I hid behind my high school and smoked pot out of a crumpled can. The second hand on the clock ticked in slow motion. Surely he could hear my pulse. The past, no matter how distant, was threaded into the present and the sergeant knew that in every timeline I was a bad, bad girl. We all are.

"You can't think of them as friends," he said finally. The muscles in his face relaxed into a near smile, and he looked less severe and more like someone's dad: thinning white hair, out-of-date glasses, pillow for an abdomen. "You have to remember that these women are in here because of choices they made." He took a seat. "They will use you and lie to you. Do you understand?"

"Yes, sir," I said. "I didn't come here to make friends." He looked into my eyes without blinking, the staring-contest equivalent of an arm-wrestling match. I lost.

❧

Jade (not her real name) waited by the doors of the Janice Weiss Education and Music Building with a vacuum and a caddy full of cleaning supplies. It was normal to have women waiting on the steps, especially the college correspondence students, eager for higher education. A Saturday in the computer lab was a productive way to pass the time, and the girls pursuing degrees tended to be model prisoners.

An inmate without her high school diploma was required to spend ten hours a week studying or she would not be allowed to purchase anything during the weekly concessions. This is where women bought candy, lip gloss, eyeliner, corn nuts, toothpaste, and blush. They worked jobs that paid anywhere from thirty-five cents to two dollars an hour; some worked in the kitchen, others the textile factory or laundry room. Jade was there, not as a student, but on janitorial duty, to wipe the desks and vacuum the carpet. But no matter how diligently she cleaned, the room would always smell of dog urine.

Hiland hosted a cell dog program called SPOT, short for Special Pet Obedience Training. Death-row dogs were rescued from the pound and brought to prison for obedience school. This type of program had spread across the American prison system like yoga across the middle class. It was a feel-good idea for the public—the dogs got a second chance at life, and the program gave the inmates an opportunity to return something positive to the community in the form of a healthy, well-socialized, and adoptable pet. Some dogs became service dogs for disabled veterans. But the real success of the program was its therapeutic value: participating inmates learned to redirect their focus from themselves to others, making the ruined carpet and occasional dog fight worth all the trouble.

Outside the curtained window, lush grass stretched from the greenhouses to the living quarters. Some of my regular students were lying on their backs in the sun, scrubs hiked up to their thighs in makeshift shorts, sleeves rolled up. The real women of Hiland Mountain were working on their tans.

I settled down at the big table while Jade wiped off my desk with disinfectant, closed open drawers with her knees, and stacked student work into the inbox. A classic Walkman rested in her breast pocket, and she had pulled her headphones down to her neck to talk. Jade moved with the beat as she talked and cleaned, and all the while, her eyes surveyed the room. This was not the kind of woman who missed details.

Jade was telling me about a woman who had been in solitary, the prison inside prison, for several months after shanking a guard. My colleagues called the Solitary Treatment Unit "the clank," and the inmates called it "the hole." Dysphemisms and dramatic nicknames were common inside, an aspect of criminal culture as familiar as the F-bomb. Who doesn't want to be just a little tougher than she really is, cleverer, a lot more stoic?

"She looks like a wolf now. Hair all crazy and shit," Jade said. "She just paces in there, day and night. You know? They haven't let anyone speak to her for a year. It's fucked up that they treat her like an animal. She's a person. She can't even talk to her mom," she said. Jade's mother had died the previous year.

"Why did she shank a guard?"

"I don't know. She's crazy?" The wolf she spoke of had sliced a guard with a weapon made from Bic razors a month before my first day. The sergeant often described the incident to scare new teachers into a state of alertness.

Skeptically, I asked, "*No one* is allowed to talk to her? Not even other women in the hole?"

"Nope," Jade said. She saw this as yet another example of how the system is cruel and stacked against the women.

Inmates normally barbarized the guards and vice versa. But they recognized the humanity in fellow inmates, even those guilty of violent and unimaginable crimes—crimes against children and loved ones. Jade too had stabbed someone, but unlike the shanked guard who walked away from the incident, Jade's victim died of sepsis two weeks after the assault. Yet Jade squirmed at the thought of her fellow inmate existing in the world without anyone to touch or talk to. I had my doubts that such punishment fit the idea of "rehabilitation," a lofty word lawmakers used when they talked about prisons. But I didn't show Jade my disapproval.

I wondered if we had conditioned ourselves only to expect the worst out of people who would forever be judged by their biggest mistake. Would we let them rehabilitate? *Perhaps it is good I am leaving soon*, I thought. Although I kept my hand near the radio whenever I was alone with an inmate—just in case—I knew I was too comfortable around the prisoners. The sergeant would have been disappointed. *You might as well give her some scissors and a metal fork*, I could imagine him saying. *You're not in control of this situation.* That was part of my problem, and the reason I didn't have a future in corrections—I *liked* Jade. She was one of the first students who joined my creative writing class, and I'd read about her past, her lovers, the death of her mother. I was no expert, but intuition told me she was one of the few felons who might never make it back to that mountain, if she could just learn to control her rage.

‿

"I just got my new breast. Want to see?" Diana announced as she slipped into the GED study room later that day, tray of cancer lunch Saran-wrapped against a Styrofoam plate—hardboiled egg, green salad, and a Red Delicious.

I looked at her chest. In felon scrubs, all breasts looked like a single, yellow shelf, but Diana's shelf had been lopsided for almost a year. She set her food on the big table by me. The other inmates who'd made their way in paid no attention, noses buried in their taped-up math books. Normally, no one ate in the education building, but Diana didn't turn any heads with this brazenness—we were all happy to see her eating. She scooted her chair close to mine and looked at me with earnest brown eyes, one drooping slightly. "How has your summer been? Are you doing okay?" she asked.

Diana had no reason to be in the education room other than to visit. She had taken several college classes, finished my own writing course, and had, in fact, decided not to write until she felt well again because the practice "stressed her out." I regretted I couldn't change her mind. She had worked for several months on a piece that contrasted Sarah Palin with her Buddhist mentor, Judith.

The nonfiction workshop was designed to engage learners in literacy through writing assignments and reading discussions. The women who enrolled, on average, wrote and read near a ninth-grade level. When the first assignment was turned in, I was surprised by Diana's narrative voice. She wrote about then governor Palin visiting Hiland to commemorate Wyatt's graduation. Wyatt was the first service dog to complete SPOT. Wyatt was being presented to a wounded Alaska veteran. The event was part of Palin's PR circuit. But Diana was conflicted during the visit; Palin supported new death penalty legislation, something that could have applied to her in the past.

Most of the ladies I'd worked with in that environment were preoccupied with themselves and their situation—understandably—and would take any opportunity to give a full defense of why they were inside and why they thought, when the facts of the circumstances were explained, that the reason they were there was not their fault. Diana didn't defend or even talk about her crime, only ever said she was a long-timer.

Diana got right down to the things that occupied her mind: What do you think God is? What does it mean to forgive? Can a person forgive herself? What is compassion? Why should I write about my past when I have so much to regret? A practicing Buddhist, she liked to discuss religious philosophy, and her quest to discover answers to unknowable questions made her not only a promising writer, but an engaging conversationalist.

I was finishing the last hours of my contract at Hiland and not planning to renew. I knew I was running out of time to ask Diana something I had been afraid to: how did you get from being a killer to the person you are today? Is it an act? She would have had the courage to ask me these questions if our roles had been reversed. But I couldn't ignore the etiquette—one should never ask about crime. It's best to wait for inmates to volunteer information. Wait and listen.

Diana's public records provided a grim account of the verifiable facts but nothing convincing about her motives. On December 9, 1994, Diana buckled her seven-year-old daughter into her car, loaded a .357 magnum, and drove from Anchorage into the night of her darkest winter. Maybe it was storming. Maybe all she could see were the thick snowflakes that whipped across her headlights. Diana said she had tunnel vision the night she drove to her victim's home, knocked on his door, and shot him once in the front, and twice in the back as he tried to run away.

Records from the 1998 appeal of her sentence surprised me with the brutality of her crime:

> The evidence presented at the sentencing hearing showed that Waggy is a deeply troubled woman with severe psychological problems. She was often depressed to the point of dysfunction. She periodically threatened to kill either herself or members of her family, other intimate friends, her employers, and her mental health counselors. She deluged the Anchorage Crisis Line with telephone calls (as many as fifty calls in a month), and she was twice hospitalized at the Alaska Psychiatric Institute.
>
> ... Wolf, for his part, came to perceive the full extent of Waggy's mental illness, and he ultimately despaired that

*Waggy would ever be able to lead a normal life or that he could maintain a relationship with her.*

*Wolf tried to end the relationship, but Waggy clung to him, hounding him with visits and telephone calls. Wolf ultimately convinced Waggy to leave Anchorage and move to Seattle to live with her mother. However, Waggy's mother was not a good nurturer, and Waggy soon returned to Alaska. Out of work and without a place to live, Waggy concluded that Wolf was to blame for all of her current difficulties because he was the one who convinced her to move to Seattle.*

Not a good nurturer? Diana said once, "My mother taught me depression, and my father taught me rage." Something was missing from the records, compelling me to ask her side of the story.

As we sat having lunch together that last Saturday, I found some nerve: I lowered my voice and said, "My contract is almost up, Diana. I won't be coming here anymore." I would miss these lunches, miss talking about the books she was reading for the book club, hearing about her daughter's cross-country trip that never seemed to end, defending my "patriarchal Christian faith."

"Will you write me?" she asked.

"Yes," I smiled. "Will you keep writing?" We both laughed. I'd been trying to talk Diana into picking up the pen again. My heart started beating rapidly. "Can I ask you something?"

"Sure."

"How did you come to be here?"

"I murdered someone."

"I know. I mean, it just seems really unlikely. I wouldn't have thought *you* could do that."

"I couldn't now. But I did," she said tersely. "And I don't really want to talk about it here." Her face was red. I'd overstepped her boundaries and we were both embarrassed. I was supposed to be on her side. Not another person judging her by the single-worst decision she ever made.

"Listen," she said after a long silence, "I will tell you my story, but not here. I want you to understand that I was a very selfish person when I came here. I spent my first three years in the hole. I was very—" she paused to find the right word, "sick."

"I understand. Thank you," I said. "So do you think you would start writing again if I got you a really cool journal?"

༄

Later that day, I sat on the cement floor of the clank, facing the slit in Felicia's cell door, and pushed through the last assignment from workshop. After dinner, I had closed the education building while the inmates went to their rooms for the evening count. This happened every twelve hours as the guards changed shifts. I took the opportunity to respond to a note in my office that explained why Felicia had missed class the previous Wednesday. Could I please bring her work to Solitary Treatment Unit? I had no idea how many women were currently there, and I wondered behind which door Jade's wolf woman hid.

Felicia and I had just a short while to talk about "place" and discuss Gretel Ehrlich's "The Solace of Open Spaces." I sat on my knees, looking through a very tiny window, and thought how the position I was in resembled prayer. Women come to solitary, also called segregation, for three reasons: correction, protection, and medication adjustment. Felicia was in the hole for protection. "Guess I don't know when to shut up," she cited as explanation.

I had been contracting for the Department of Corrections for the majority of Felicia's sentence and still had no idea if I was capable of reaching her as an educator.

Beyond the small rectangular opening, silhouetted against the light, Felicia looked like a very thin Janice Joplin figure. She stood like someone a bit wasted, but fierce, ready to get scrappy at the smallest disrespect. Humongous hair frizzed around her face and stole my attention as she dropped quickly to her knees in front of me. Her eyes filled the meal slit and crinkled.

The education director had warned me that Felicia lied. Often. So when Felicia told me that she had eight children, I didn't believe her—she seemed far too young and hard. But tucked against her breast she carried a picture of herself surrounded by eight kids. She'd showed it to me once.

STU pulsed with the dim light of a 1950s detective movie. It smelled like someone had been sleeping all night in the basement— like breath and rust. Concrete floors and off-white walls held gray doors that slid open only by a switch in the control room.

I said to Felicia, "It really is like the movies. I'll have to write about this."

"You probably won't get around to it," she said. "Spend all your time talking about the things you're going to write about." Her eyes crinkled again, and I imagined her toothy smile behind the heavy door.

Felicia was tough. Tough like a construction worker, but pretty like someone they would whistle at. Her lovely Little Mermaid voice with the ghetto-prominent affectation no longer sounded awkward to me. For a minute we exchanged verbal jabs, and I forgot our respective roles. We were simply two women happy to see each other. After many months working together, Felicia had finally quit trying to shock me.

"So Diana spent three years in a room just like this?" I asked, peeking around her to the tiny cube complete with a toilet and twin bed.

"You watch it Ms. Mary. Waggy's just another hustler, like all us bitches. Everybody wants something."

"You know what I think, Felicia?"

"That we're all a bunch of puppies and kittens?"

"No."

"That we all just need a big hug?" She continued mocking me.

"I think you're full of shit."

"Ha! Now you get it!" Her laugh was the yip of a wise little fox, swaggering from the coop in a cloud of white feathers.

❧

The class I had led for the past two years was called Telling Stories: A Workshop of Creative Nonfiction. It was my first solo teaching experience and had consequences I didn't expect—students revealed so much of themselves to me that I felt close to them. The nature of the genre lent itself to memoir and confession, especially for the new writer who often is compelled to explore the most harrowing and emotional events of her past. More practiced writers try to avoid what I once heard referred to as "the dead grandmother essay." As writers read, write, and study the craft, they move away from the bathos of the white-hot emotional core. Many believe that writing to heal has its own quiet place in the privacy of diaries. In prison though, Grandma didn't just die, she was shot. She was cut. She was a pedophile. She was a saint. She was the only person who ever believed in you.

One Wednesday, not long after I first started teaching, no one but Penny McLinn (not her real name) showed up to the workshop. Together we decided to do a series of writing exercises from *Tell It Slant*, the textbook that, by some miracle, the Department of Corrections agreed to supply. Penny wrote about her sister getting hit by a tow truck while they played in the snow as children. I wrote a quick dialogue I'd overheard two women shout back and forth in the cafeteria. Penny wrote about being raped by her psychologist when she was fourteen years old.

We worked in the "quiet room," a ten-by-ten office originally meant to be a storage closet. The walls were all blue, and the only furnishings were a file cabinet and the two desks where we sat. A map of the world hung above the desk Penny used. She finished her exercises and stared at me, tapping the desk and waiting to share. She was between twenty-one and thirty (it's hard to tell when a woman is fresh off a serious meth addiction), had frank blue eyes, a blonde bob, and high cheekbones.

"Ms. Mary, I don't know anyone who talks like you," she said when I finished reading my sketch. As she read hers, her paper trembled. She dropped information bombs like, "and that's when my dad died," and "my mom told everyone we were messing around together." Meaning her mom had falsely accused Penny and her dad of having a sexual affair.

Penny's crime was probably small compared to the injustices she suffered as a girl. The world map above her head was mockery, full of oceans and palaces and strange lands that most of us can someday, if we so choose, make our oyster, but for her it would remain an abstract idea. The world she came from was small and ugly, populated with the men that rape you when they are meant to help and the women who accuse you of asking for it.

We talked about scene. We talked about audience. I hoped I was doing more good than harm.

"I know people like you don't know what to do with me," she said. "I know most people don't really care about my dad dying, and they don't know how to take me being raped."

I wanted to say the right thing, but I didn't know what that was.

"Remember what you were saying about audience?" she asked. "See my Audience . . ."—she said it with a capital A—"my Audience is people like me. There are people out there and in here who are just like me. That's why I want to write. I know there are. I have to get it out."

*That's why you should write, Penny*—I wanted to say—because people don't know how to take you, or this prison, or some of the things that are hardest to look at and understand.

What was Penny's crime? Drug related. Most are. After reading heartbreaking student work, I wondered how much drug and alcohol use was a form of self-medication in response to trauma. Penny did a lot of drugs, even when she was pregnant, and even with her three-year-old daughter in the room. Eventually, Penny was released to a halfway house, for the briefest time, and then escorted in handcuffs right back to Hiland because she used drugs again.

"But it's not my fault," she said. "Things were so fucked up in there, and OCS won't let me see my babies. I just couldn't cope." This excuse—any excuse—would have troubled me at one time, but I'd been instructed on what psychologists call the *victim stance*: some people who commit heinous crimes justify bad behavior by remembering their own trauma.

The victim stance is such a common phenomenon that prisons develop therapeutic cognitive-behavioral programs to address that kind of thinking. In his article "Rethinking 'Don't Blame the Victim': The Psychology of Victimhood," Dr. Ofer Zur explains, "The victim stance is a powerful one. The victim is always morally right, neither responsible nor accountable, and forever entitled to sympathy." After having read the autobiographies of women in Hiland, I knew that many began their lives as victims of physical, emotional, and sexual abuse. Long after they had victims of their own, "victim" was still how they identified themselves.

❧

Animals pace when put in a cage. The only time I went to the zoo, I watched a wolverine run the border of its enclosure for twenty minutes. Even while its body raced, its catatonic eyes glazed over like a blacked-out drunk. It ran and ran and I moved on.

In 1994 Diana Waggy began three years of pacing back and forth in STU, stewing in her own madness. Other long-timers remember her from the dark days; they said she rocked back and forth in her cell and growled like something feral.

"I remember the pacing, walking in circles," Diana said, "but not growling."

During the last week of my contract, I arranged to meet with Diana privately for an interview. She had to sign an official press release and would be required to notify her victim's family if anything I wrote about her was published. Among other things, I wanted to know if what appeared to be Diana's rehabilitation was really possible.

I believed that it embarrassed Diana to tell me what she had been like. Her droopy brown eyes brimmed with tenderness and regret, but anyone would wonder if there was some sectioned off part of her mind, a dark cell maybe, where something wild rattled its cage. During her first appeal, the defense and the government offered differing views on Diana's prospects for rehabilitation. Both experts concluded that Diana suffered from borderline personality disorder, which one medical journal describes as "a condition in which people have long-term patterns of unstable or turbulent emotions, such as feelings about themselves and others. These inner experiences often cause them to take impulsive actions and have chaotic relationships." As often happens, Diana's mental illness was properly addressed for the first time only when she was in prison. With her severe depression and anxiety treated, she displayed no violent tendencies.

Yet it was not surprising when Diana's appeal judge remained unconvinced she was a good candidate for a shorter sentence. Alaska prosecutes the criminally insane to the fullest extent of the law. And Diana had murdered one of their own. The opinion of the court was delivered by Judge Mannheimer:

> A person who is mentally ill may not always have the same moral blameworthiness as other people. By the same token, a person's mental illness may make them more dangerous and less susceptible to rehabilitative measures than other people. Here, all the experts agreed that Waggy suffered from serious, debilitating mental illnesses—illnesses that made it very difficult for her to function normally in society. Judge Cutler declared that, given this psychiatric testimony, a maximum sentence was not appropriate. Nevertheless, Judge Cutler found that Waggy deliberately drove to Wasilla to kill Wolf because he would no longer support her, either emotionally or financially. For this reason, Judge Cutler analogized the slaying to "the worst . . . domestic violence murder," and she felt obliged to emphasize the sentencing goals of deterrence and reaffirmation of societal norms.
>
> Having reviewed the record, we cannot say that Judge Cutler's sentencing decision is clearly mistaken. See *McClain v. State*, 519 P.2d 811, 813-14 (Alaska 1974). We therefore uphold Waggy's sentence.
>
> The judgment of the superior court is AFFIRMED.

"Luckily for everyone, people can change," Diana told me during our interview. "Unfortunately, I didn't change direction until after I murdered someone."

"Long-timers learn to be quiet," she continued, "because no one likes to be in the hole."

Two years after she made it to the open population, she still had obsessive thoughts, an agitated mind, the same consciousness that loaded a .357 and drove to Wasilla. But eventually, the blackness of her tunnel vision dilated enough for her to reach for the phone book. *Buddhists always look calm*, she thought. *Maybe that can help me*. It was 1999 and the only listing under Buddhist was the Anchorage Zen Community. No one answered. She left a message: *Please help me*. Insert the catalyst for change: Diana's mentor, Judith, cofounder of the AZC.

In the beginning, Diana told me, she filled their brief visits with a lot of complaining. She didn't want to be in prison, didn't feel she deserved to be there, thought she should have been helped before she killed a man. Society owed it to Diana and her daughter to save her from herself before she shot Wolf. After all, she did reach out for help, did call help lines, friends, even a Baptist church to ask her pastor if she and her daughter could stay with him. She knew he had a room.

By 1999, the year Judith came to Diana, something big was shifting in her thinking. Was it her time in the hole that caused it? Was it the realization that no one would help her? That her life continued to go on and on even after she lost everything—her daughter, her best friend, her freedom?

Judith sensed something sincere in Diana's plea for help. From the beginning, despite her complaining, Diana acknowledged her crime. Judith began the slow process of teaching her the tenets of Buddhism: compassion and wisdom. For Judith, the first step was to help Diana see what *actually* happened. Not what she wanted to happen, or wished had happened, but what really happened.

"I remember her saying there is no alternate universe where you're not in prison. You are here. You have to deal with what is happening right now," Diana said, describing an early visit from Judith.

"I don't understand something, Diana," I said. "How do you teach compassion? I mean, you either care or you don't."

"That's not true. I didn't care about anything but myself back then. I was very boring. A typical narcissistic criminal. But if you imitate compassion for long enough, if you make yourself ask people how they are doing, and take the time to listen to them, eventually you start to really care. You actually want to know."

I wondered if it could be that simple, that compassion could be achieved through hard work or habit. If empathy (the cornerstone of compassion) is the intellectual and emotional awareness of another's thoughts, feelings, and behavior, it follows that someone with an untreated personality disorder might have a hard time achieving this. Was it possible that the shift in Diana's character was a combination of proper medication and exposure to positive role models?

"Do you think Judith and Buddhism led you to being a compassionate and good person, or would you have healed on your own?" I asked Diana. To my surprise, she began to cry. This was only the second time I'd seen her come apart. The first time was when she said good-bye to her favorite SPOT dog when she went to the city jail for five months of chemotherapy. Her prognosis was not positive.

"It's unconditional friendship on her part. Judith accepted me the way I was. The way I am. A murderer. A nothing. I did have compassion—for my daughter, for animals, but not for myself. And I lost everything, my friends, most of my family." She paused for a minute. I pushed a box of tissues toward her. She blew her nose and smiled.

"What is it?" I asked. "What are you thinking?"

"After a meeting with Judith I was worried. In Buddhism, death is a very important day. I told her I didn't even have anyone to claim my body when I die. Judith said, 'I will claim your body.' And I know she will."

"What will she do with it?" I asked.

"I practiced my own death before I started chemotherapy," Diana said. "I wrote a will. I signed Do Not Resuscitate papers. Another AZC teacher, Cindy, showed me a picture of the view from her cabin. That's where they'll spread my ashes."

Diana will be up for parole in twelve years. She practices for that day too. It's one thing to love compassionately in a controlled environment, to trust in its power to heal a dark heart, but I wondered if Judith's and Cindy's friendship would go beyond the walls of the institution, if they would meet her on the other side of its doors.

❧

When I came home late after my interview with Diana, my husband greeted me in the entryway and asked how my day had been. I always felt lucky when I came home from Hiland, thankful I wasn't addicted to drugs, that my mother wasn't abusive, that I had two big brothers for surrogate parents, that I was married to a kind man. I sat on the stairs and untied my shoes, telling him about saying good-bye to Diana. I asked if he would be comfortable with me giving her our address so I could continue to correspond with her. He leaned against the doorway with his arms crossed over his chest.

"Why do you want to write her?" he asked.

"I don't know. Because I want to encourage her to keep writing. And I care about her." But I filed the question away for later because I wasn't sure if I believed my answer. I needed to think about it.

"Do you think this is smart?" he asked. *Are you out of your mind?* his expression read. I handed him my shoes and he put them on the shoe rack. The sergeant would be shaking his head. *Professional boundaries, lady.*

"Be careful." He offered his hand and pulled me to my feet.

"Safety first," I promised. "She's not an animal, you know. She's a normal woman who had a really bad day. *Seventeen* years ago."

He leaned in to kiss me. I'm sure I smelled like Hiland: disinfectant, dog pee, and mold. He wouldn't miss his wife reeking of institution. "I'm serious," he said. He was a man who checked the windows frequently and bought a door reinforcement that he tucked under the knob each night before bed.

"Look, I'm not asking if she can move in. She's not even up for parole for at least twelve years. I don't know. It just *feels* right."

He rolled his eyes at my choice of words and turned to lock the door.

❧

I arranged to meet Judith at a café shortly after interviewing Diana. I was nervous. I had this idea that Zen masters possessed exceptional human insight and worried that she might understand me better than I was comfortable with.

Judith dressed comfortably in a thin white shirt and loose blue pants. She had pinned a pink heart to the center of her chest that matched her pink sandals. I remember that detail because she told me that she once met a man who said he knew how to see auras, and she thought she'd give it a try. "I realized that it is not auras I was looking for," she said. "I want to see inside people's hearts."

It struck me that Judith retained the best kind of interest in others. She didn't bear the detached serenity I'd expected; instead she wore the expression of a woman who might break into laughter at any moment. She conveyed easiness and mirth, characteristics that encouraged comfort and openness.

Judith had once worked for the McLaughlin Youth Center before she started volunteering at the correctional facility. I had never met with someone associated with Hiland outside of the prison. After the initial small talk, I asked, "Would you be friends outside if Diana ever gets released?"

No hesitation. "Yes. I would have boundaries. She couldn't live with me. But I would do all the things I do with friends. Go for walks, go to the movies."

I shared with Judith that I didn't feel I was good with boundaries and that the longer I worked at Hiland, the more I empathized with the inmates.

"People have funny ideas about prison," she said. I knew exactly what she meant, my own having been formed by television. Everybody is dangerous. Everybody deserves to be there. And if you can't reconcile that reality, you might just be soft on crime.

"I once visited a school for Career Day to talk to kids about working in the McLaughlin Youth Center. I'll never forget afterward this little girl came up and asked me if they have birthdays in there." She pulled her lips into a half smile then sipped her tea. I laughed at the anecdote but recognized the implications—when someone gets locked up, sectioned off from society because of how dangerous they are, one doesn't think about them blowing out candles, about their mothers sending them care packages, about that one day etched in the permanent calendars of all the people who love them.

"I think you know what I mean," she said. "You realize quickly that these are just people in trouble."

❧

Not long after I quit working at Hiland, I met a woman whose daughter was killed in a botched drug deal. The three men present at her murder had separate trials. The process took years. After the last verdict, the mother quit answering her phone and volunteering at the place where I worked. When I checked on her, she said, "We lost. The last guy was found not guilty. I don't understand how someone can just watch my daughter get killed and still be found not guilty."

"I'm so sorry."

"I just can't believe it. I haven't been able to eat or sleep. I'm trying to be strong, but *we lost*."

When I worked at Hiland, I didn't have tough conversations with the other victims, the victims of the crimes. I thought anew of the penal system's lofty words. *Correction* benefits the criminal, and *rehabilitation* serves society, but *justice* is so the victim doesn't have to lose anymore.

When Diana finally does leave Hiland, in ashes or on foot, I hope she'll have a safe place to go. I'll still be her friend. I still think that the women inside need tenderness and mercy, but I don't doubt that Diana is exactly where she needs to be right now.

My favorite moment with Diana was during a performance by the Hiland Mountain String Orchestra, the only prison ensemble of its kind in the United States. The inmates prepared for the finale. The piece, "Toss the Feathers," was an Irish folk tune, traditionally played with a whistle and a fiddle. The song was to be a combined effort of the advanced, intermediate, and beginning musicians.

The first few notes wobbled forth timidly.

"What's the difference between a violin and a fiddle?" the maestro called to the audience.

"How you play it!" we screamed, and all the strings joined in at once.

Diana sat beside me, her face free of guilt and worry; she leaned forward and began to clap with every other woman in the gymnasium. Penny McLinn, a few seats past us, caught my eyes and grinned. The frantic wail of the violins pushed against the rafters. I thought the roof was cracking. We were ascending. All of the pain and joy of four hundred women rattled against the low notes and fluttered with the highs. There was no past or future, just the thunder of hands, the drum of feet stomping out the old isle jig.

# PART THREE

*Your pure sadness that wants help is the secret cup.*
*Listen to the moan of a dog for its master.*
*That whining is the connection.*

—*Rumi*

# STRONGHOLD

On another day we will walk this path again like it's a dream. Cottonwood drift will line the ground like a wedding run, the fireweed will don purple blossoms, and Peter will be my husband. But right now it's late in April of our first year together, and the trails are colorless. Last year's grasses, muddy straw, line the bare woods.

Arm-in-arm, Peter escorts me to his favorite beach in Anchorage. This trek was once his private ceremony, a way for him to quietly celebrate his birthday. We reveal ourselves piecemeal, still so new to each other that we have only exposed the very best features of our personalities. He does not yet know about my brother. I do not want to tell him I am afraid of heights, afraid of oceans, afraid of sleep and silence and empty houses.

The path down to the beach is steep, and the fall long. Cottonwoods squat along the bluff's edge like gargoyles, knotted and hard, molded by the sea wind into otherworldly shapes. The spirits within are the ghosts of old warriors—weathered skin and arthritic hands, sentinels watching for dark riders.

I scoot down the path behind Peter, clutching at the remains of last year's foliage like it's rope. Like it will save me. Please don't turn around, I think. He does and offers up his hand so that I might balance against him. At the bottom, gray mudflats stretch on and on into Cook Inlet, home of one of the world's most powerful tides. The water is so low we could walk across the bay if the wet sand wasn't a quick grave. The mud has claimed people who wandered too far, shackled and drowned them. But not me. Not today.

Ahead of me, Peter walks onto the still-firm sand. My eyes adore him, his broad shoulders—peasant shoulders he calls them. The wind plasters his clothes to his runner's legs, and he is a steeple, a tower. Not me. I live in the rickety body of haunted women. I wish

I had a quiet mind and steady legs. I spent last spring in a motel room as stuffy as a coffin watching my mother turn into an old woman. We waited for Seth's body to be cremated, to gather his ashes, his gun, his ghost.

Peter turns his back to the ocean and pulls me to his chest. We are new, and there is so much fire, so much heat it reached me through a grief I couldn't pray or drink away. I would dream at night of the people I love hanging from the ceiling, rocking back and forth like a metronome. I'd wake thinking someday, not on a rope or by a gun, but someday I will disappear.

But I'm not thinking about that now, nor am I thinking of the sandpaper wind, strong enough to whittle a woman into skeleton. Instead, I wonder if Peter can feel the quickness of my pulse, and I wonder if he will bring me here on his next birthday. I'm thinking too about how much I love the sound of the human heartbeat. How Peter's chest is big enough to shield me. How love shelters, coaxes, lights.

The ocean and sky bend to a soft, gray crest, an unending horizon. On the bluffs above, watchwoods lean into the jagged edge, towering over a tide that marches toward us on wet boots. No matter. For now, I can forget that even at our finest—bodies hard, strength united, two forms fastened—we are soft and unchampioned.

I press my body all the way into Peter's and hold on.

# THE ORIGIN OF LIGHT

A scrap of paper fell from a student's display board as she walked out of the Learning Resource Center, distracting me from the conversation at hand. I leaned against the pay phone outside of the university's writing center where I tutored, listening to my mom talk about the weather back home. If there were more relevant news, she would save it for the end of the conversation or not share it at all. I wanted to talk about my brother until I understood what happened. I called my mom almost every day. I told myself it was to check up on her, remind her that she still had two living children, but the truth is I was running out of people who could bear the guilt I wallowed in. The real conversations burned inside me: *the guilt, the guilt, Mom—*

My mother could avoid guilt. She took refuge behind the facts: Seth had struggled with depression. He was a logger who had lost his leg at age twenty-four, and during that same colossally horrible job, one member of the crew, a woman he cared for, died of propane poisoning. Seth was exposed to the same gas and afterward resembled Lennie Small; he felt responsible. He lost the lawsuit and declared bankruptcy. He spent the last fourteen years of his life in a scat-encrusted shack, terrified of losing more.

Anyone listening in on our pleasant conversation would never guess my brother had killed himself three weeks earlier. My mom chattered about Whip and Judy, the blacksmith and his wife, who lived at Mile 22. They'd been visiting her just about every day. It was a little like talking to a person from a different era, or maybe a character from historical fiction. She lived in a small, rural town, and her friends had occupations like "knife maker" and "railroad worker," and Postmistress Martha kept everyone abreast of the latest gossip.

I listened to her for a while and tried to contain my own bad mood. The strip of paper that had fallen from the student's display board caught my attention again. It was a little scrap about the length of a finger, pastel and distinct on the sea of beige Berber. It held a command written in the round, bubbly penmanship that I associated with missionaries and elementary schoolteachers. It said, "Be the light." I imagined the kind of person who could write a sentence like that, someone who ran marathons and held intangibles like "bliss" or "serenity" as daily goals.

I picked it up and considered the hideous weight of that single imperative sentence. As I said good-bye and started back toward the writing center, another wave of students passed the pay phone, vibrating with laughter and enthusiastic conversation, pulling books from their bags without ever stopping or slowing down.

I was barely there, I knew that much. I watched them as if from a great distance.

❧

The phoenix lives in Arabia near a deep, cool well. Each morning, as dawn turns the early sky pink and gold, it bathes in the clear water and sings so mellifluously that the sun-god stops to listen and weeps. Only one phoenix can exist at a time.

When the well dries, when the dawn brings only charged clouds, when the horizon vibrates with thunder and the phoenix feels death approaching, it builds a nest of aromatic wood and sets itself on fire. I had to stop worrying about you for a little while, Seth. I didn't know what could happen.

A new phoenix will spring from the pyre and embalm the ashes of its predecessor in an egg of myrrh. The new phoenix will be strong. It will carry the burden of its body into the City of the Sun.

❧

In most cases it's the family who cleans up the mess, the bits of hair and teeth. My living brother and I removed the sofa, but a family friend, Becky, spared us the worst of it. Still, decisions must be made and quickly.

*Mary Beth, what should I do with the brain?* Becky asked. The paramedics took the body, but a large piece of the brain had fallen behind the couch.

I don't know, Becky. I can't think about it right now. Can you just do something with it?

*Maybe I should have buried it, or something.* Becky whispered to me at the wake. *The brain, I mean. I wrapped it in a plastic bag and I put it in the trash can.*

I can't think about it right now, Becky.

For months I didn't drink. I exercised and took care not to abuse my body. I sought counseling. Yet grief stripped my memory of day-to-day details, and I recall little, with the exception of an undergraduate poetry workshop.

The small class sat at a round table. I faced a nineteen-year-old Cure fan—thin, dyed-black hair, tall boots, and tight, tight jeans. He read aloud in rhyming couplets of feeling hollow inside, of ravens swooping, falling, "announcing" the corpse. Black roses and Armageddon every Thursday night that semester. I could indulge in the angst-ridden Sylvia Plath tributes, the insincere fascination with mortality, but some nights that boy wore a white T-shirt with fake blood around the collar, a theatrical garment, red-glue droplets spilling down his chest. It whispered to me, *My head is gone. My head is gone.*

❧

There was a time when everything was still and all of the spirits slept. Australian Aboriginals call it *Dreamtime*. The planets revolved around the sun, and the moons around the planets, and the cosmos spiraled outward. The universe moved like a machine, but all of its inhabitants were still. The Sun Mother woke first. She came to Earth and walked in all directions and in all the places that she treaded, spirits rose. She penetrated caves and crevices with bright light; she glided north, her heat melting the ice, forming the rivers and streams of the world. All living creatures watched her in awe as she moved west across the sky.

I think we were there, Seth. And when she finally disappeared beneath the horizon, we were terrified, thinking she had abandoned us. Some of the others froze in fear, not moving all night, wondering if the end of time had come or if they were having a nightmare. But after only a few hours of darkness, the Sun Mother came from the east, luminous and comforting. The Earth's children learned to expect her coming and going and were no longer afraid.

෧

In some dreams Seth hangs from the ceiling like a brightly colored piñata. In other dreams he walks in circles like a zombie, his .30-06 rifle strapped to his back. I must confiscate his gun and make him human again. Sometimes he morphs into my husband or my mother or my best friend, and I have to save them all, but I'm always too late. I'm told this isn't narcissism, just magical thinking, a manifestation of survivor's guilt.

*The most tragic part about depression-related suicides,* one psychologist said, *is they are entirely preventable.* In most cases properly treated depression will get better eventually. We've come a long way with medications. *If we can just get the patient to hang on.*

෧

I read of a woman who is terrified of the Vincent Thomas Bridge in Los Angeles. The temptation to throw herself off is so great that she moved across the country to gain a safe proximity. I feel that way about darkness. The same empty room, plain with lamplight and white walls, fills with ghosts and bones the minute I flip the switch.

Light is an Alaska industry; we weigh it like gold, track it like stocks. I had thought winter solstice was the bell curve of suicide death, but actually, most suicides occur near the equinoxes, before winter and before summer. On average, 1 percent of people in the United States commit suicide. In Alaska, where Seth and I grew up, the average is double.

Winter mornings, I'd swallow vitamin D tablets and sit under a special light meant to ward off seasonal affective disorder. The radio, the news, the daily paper's weather reports announced highs in the upper thirties, lows in the midtwenties, and four minutes and fifty-five seconds less daylight.

ॐ

My mom's friend Whip died suddenly of a heart attack that December. Within hours his wife, Judy, drove her car into Kenai Lake, which was just beginning to freeze. The Moose Pass town hall filled for their wake and Whip's best friend, Virgil the knife maker, read Longfellow's "The Village Blacksmith" to the stunned residents. It had been almost twenty years since Whip and Judy had moved from Fairbanks to Moose Pass after their own son's suicide.

After the service a small group of us headed to the lakeshore behind Whip and Judy's house. Virgil and Judy's sisters cut open the plastic bags holding the remains and I will never forget this, Seth: Whip's ashes were black and Judy's nearly white. Before we left, Virgil threw Whip's hammer into the water, but I didn't see it ripple. I was watching all their expressions because they looked so hopeful, like they were expecting the catharsis of ceremony. Except Mom, she was looking for you.

ॐ

In the beginning, there was only the Holy Darkness.

And it was the Darkness that released the Holy Light. God formed vessels to hold this light, but there was a miscalculation—the vessels were not as strong as God had thought. They split and shattered, a cataclysm so devastating that it birthed the suffering universe. Light and ruins and maybe even God Himself tumbled down toward the realm of matter.

Kabbalist mystics say we can help God by freeing the Light, raising the sparks back to their original unity. *Tikkun Olam*. Restore the broken whole and heal the world.

❧

Edith, a sixty-seven-year-old woman from Nebraska, saw the Light. She moved through "levels," where the souls of the living "work things out"; she only came back because her grandson would have been orphaned at age seven. Edith had never read Dante's *Divine Comedy* or the *Tibetan Book of the Dead*; she'd rarely left the farm. "If it weren't for the boy," she wrote, "I'd have stayed in the Light."

Another man coded for one minute and fifty-three seconds. He emerged on a beach, felt grains of sand between his toes, and spotted a thatched hut in the distance. Inside, his deceased parents looked fifty years younger. They touched him. He felt their touch. He was reunited with his best friend. Then the Light came from under a doorway and drew him in.

When I mentioned that the scriptures of my faith did nothing to soothe my grief, a counselor suggested that I research near-death experiences, an activity that comforted her when her own mother committed suicide. Since then, I've read hundreds of accounts from people who returned after being pronounced dead, and I see two common threads: when the dead see the Light they feel as though they are returning to something better; they often express frustration that there is no sufficient way to describe the unity they experienced.

"It is like a chair trying to understand a table," one woman tried to explain, or it's like trying to explain algebra to a chair"—she abandoned the metaphor—"the body just isn't big enough to hold the knowledge. The brain isn't adequate."

The vessels are not as strong as God thought.

❧

Creation stories have false beginnings. They actually start in the middle, where there was already Word, already God, already forces in motion.

Seth's suicide is my before-and-after point, the catalyst that pushed me out of East Anchorage and into graduate school, the single event that made me realize my life could not go on as it had been.

Seth had called me the night before he killed himself. He sounded confused and spoke in a low rumble, "I messed up real bad. I messed up." I didn't ask what he meant. I didn't say the right thing. The weeks and months that followed were some of the worst of my life, but they formed me and still form me.

The Book of Job, considered a book of wisdom, opens with God and Satan in dialogue. God claims Job is a perfect servant, and Satan asserts that Job is only faithful because God has given him a blessed life. In the chapters that follow, God reclaims all Job's blessings—his wife, his children, his possessions—to prove something, the reader assumes. Job is often cited as the Judeo-Christian answer to Suffering.

When he calls down to speak to Job from a "whirlwind," God doesn't say *why* He caused Job to suffer; instead He asks Job a rhetorical question, "Where were you when I laid the foundations of the Earth?" as though the answer to suffering is threaded into the act of creation, and part of Job's ignorance lies in his humanity. *Word and Light reside in God*, the Book of John explains. *God sends the Light into the darkness, and the darkness cannot comprehend it.*

e~

The first children had no memory of light. They knew the world by other senses, heard the trickle of water, felt jagged edges of rock, smelled the minerals of the cavern walls. They tasted the slime and cold of the creatures they ate, and they were content.

After a long darkness (long after the first mother disintegrated), after thousands of dreams, so many dreams that he couldn't determine waking from sleep, the boy sensed something. He tried to tell his sister what he saw. *What does it feel like?* she asked. *Taste like?* But there were no words yet for illumination, shape, color. He could only describe how the light filled him with longing. He tried to walk toward it, but he didn't know where it came from. He grew obsessive looking for its origin.

One night, while sister slept, brother found the source. It seeped from a small crack in his hand. When he pulled his skin taut, the light increased. He nudged and pulled his skin until it split the length of his palm. The cavern's creatures drew near; he saw their shapes and colors. He rolled back the skin of his hand and forearm to release more. He looked for a while at the cave walls stretching into the darkness, endless as time. How could he know there was anything else?

The boy peeled back skin until his hand lit the cavern like a torch. While the boy worked off his flesh, his sister slept by the bare, white bones of their mother. Sinew by sinew he unraveled his muscle, shedding his body in one glorious purge. He was the first to see his own blood and beauty. He was the first to *see* and to leave the world full of light.

# THREADBARE

Jason Wenger started his Bronco and rested against the driver's seat. It was December 2, 2007, and the thermometers in Anchorage read nine degrees Fahrenheit. Jason's breath would have been visible in the cold if it weren't so dark. He might have prayed while he waited for the engine to warm, hands folded in his lap and chin tucked against the gold cross he always wore. Perhaps that is what Christopher Erin Rogers Jr. saw when he approached the driver's side window with a loaded gun—a man in prayer.

At Jason's funeral, his father asked attendees, "Are you ready for Christ? Jason might not have been. Are you ready?" Naturally, some of Jason's friends were appalled at the question. They knew it would have been so easy to find something nice to say about Jason instead. He worked for a nonprofit helping people with disabilities. Jason himself said, "I believe in personal civil service." He thought it was his duty as a servant and writer to be "an active member in the community and world." He wanted to help people take care of their earthly and very real needs. The word the Hebrews used to describe God's love—*agape* in Greek—translates to *caritas* in Latin, or "charity."

Anyone could have been killed that morning (the police called it the most dangerous day in Anchorage), but it was Jason Wenger on his way to church. Perhaps his father's question was not prose-lytizing so much as a desperate sort of self-soothing: his son was gone, but this was Christ's beneficent plan. It had to be. I understand his father's hope, or might if it were my son so violently and permanently taken. Or maybe the opposite is true, and I would no longer cling to any belief but choose instead to put my faith in Justice. Or nothing.

But justice and grief are not what burden me. Although we shared a small city, friends, and a finite writing community, I never met Jason or his father. I didn't go to his funeral or pray for the Wenger family. But I did know Jason's killer and other hard men, damaged men. I know the place where their lives interlocked with each other and intersected with friends and victims and a thousand others who they will never know but touch all the same. What concerns me is the notion of Design.

&

The Thread of Destiny, a proverb with roots in Chinese and Japanese folklore, holds that we are connected to everyone we will meet by imperceptible strings. In some stories, we are tied at the ankles; in others, the gods carefully loop invisible twine around our pinky fingers, tethering us to our lovers, our husbands, our killers. The threads may tangle or grow taut, but they will never break.

I feel like two women: one grown and grounded, the other still twentysomething with little education, few job prospects, and no health care. The grown woman is safe, maintains healthy familial relationships, is charitable. The other is in danger, a daughter of alcoholics and often in the company of predators. Two women. Two tangles of string. Two fates.

Recently, a Christian friend was trying to change my stance on a political matter. She made a scripture-based argument, and I made a scripture-based counterargument.

"No offense," she said, "but with everything you have shared with me about your past, I know you were never taught *how* to interpret scripture."

I have a deep respect for my friend but feel that some of her points of view are the product of a privileged life, an upbringing of which I'm a little jealous and a little proud to have avoided.

&

In 2004, Theadose "Theo" Merculief was a pretty good-looking young man: midtwenties, brunet, cute face, lean build, like a short Dave Matthews with a lot more freckles and a lot less talent. The Village Inn servers liked him, especially the females. Some said he was an efficient employee, others called him lazy. On this day, he leaned against the counter, moving slowly and only when absolutely necessary. Theo's outfit was mostly clean, unlike his coworker Brian's, whose chef coat was covered in egg and bacon fat and grill butter. Brian was a round man and so much bigger than scrawny Theo that, side by side, they looked like the number 10.

"You're a dirty motherfucker," Theo said to make conversation. There were only four orders in, but the restaurant was filling quickly. Brian looked at Theo's white coat, nearly spotless apron, and snorted. He turned the sausage patties over with a spatula and checked the breakfast orders again.

"Let me tell you something, man," Brian started. He was about a decade older than Theo and thought of himself as a mentor of sorts. "I get dirty because I work hard. You look at my station. It's clean, stocked. I'm ready for the next rush. You can't handle that shit," he said, and moved the sausage patties to a plate of hash browns and eggs.

The men had been flipping pancakes together at the Village Inn for nearly a year. They agreed on the big things—that omelets should be rolled, not folded; that people who made too many special requests were assholes; and that the only person you can really count on in life is yourself.

After Theo and Brian caught up with orders, they would likely help Erin with dishes or prep work. Erin Rogers wasn't just their coworker; he was also Theo's roommate. The three men didn't just share cigarette breaks by the dumpsters out back. At the shift's end, they might share drinks or drugs, pot or pills, mushrooms or anything else available. Garbage partiers, Brian called it.

"Order up, sweetheart," Brian said, just loud enough to be heard in the dining room.

I enter here, twenty-three years old and sticky with waffle leftovers. I smelled like a waitress, like food and dishwater and ammonia. I smelled the way my mother smelled twenty years earlier when she was a waitress at the Bamboo Room in Haines. The cash wadded in my apron pocket would go to cigarettes and rent and just barely making ends meet. If there was any money left at all, I would spend it on Brian. I was in love.

Shortly after meeting him, I decided Brian was a wounded teddy bear, the kind some kid really loved, dragged to the playground, and buckled into the seat next to him. A rip in the side, a button missing where the eye should be. He was blond-haired and blue-eyed, reckless and selfish, too old for me. He didn't like rules or labels or cops. By his scruffy red beard, big shoulders, and belly, it was clear he'd let go of himself. At thirty-seven, he thought he was too old to try new things, to change the things about his life that he wasn't happy with, but mostly he just didn't believe it possible. At twenty-three, I thought I could fix that.

&#8766;

I'd first met Erin one afternoon when I'd given Theo a ride home after the morning shift. He stood on the lawn trimming a lilac tree and looking like a missing member of Pearl Jam. He was tall and slender with shoulder-length hair, wavy and dirty blond. He wore dark jeans, an old T-shirt, and a ratty flannel wrapped around his waist. This would have been before his brief stint as Village Inn prep cook. Erin was working for a landscaping company then and had set out to beautify Theo's yard. He had straightened the mailbox, gathered the beer cans and other trash. He raked years of leaves. Erin was a fixer.

When Brian and Theo went inside to share a joint, I introduced myself to Erin, but he wouldn't talk. He was painfully shy. I could see his discomfort and couldn't bear the awkwardness of it. "I love lilac trees," I babbled. "I love lilacs. I could smell them from two blocks away. It's my mom's favorite tree. My favorite color, actually."

Erin looked at me and looked at the front door. Why didn't Brian come out and take me away?

"I don't smoke pot. It makes me too serious," I said, feeling like I needed to defend myself for not going inside. "Do you like this tree?"

"It has bugs."

"Bugs suck. I'm just going to wait in the truck," I said.

But the next day Erin surprised me and Brian with an unannounced visit to the apartment we shared. I invited Erin inside. He sat on the loveseat in our tiny living room, his long limbs drawn close to his body as though he was afraid to take up too much space. Green stains smeared his knees and his scent promised grass, and sweat, and entire afternoons outdoors.

A long, uncomfortable silence descended on the cramped apartment, to which Brian seemed oblivious.

"I brought you seeds," Erin finally said. He stood and pulled a rolled-up plastic bag from his pants. Brian looked away from the TV for the first time. He probably thought that Erin was pulling something interesting from the plastic bag. But it wasn't weed. Erin had brought me a handful of mixed seeds from the most fragrant flowers that could be grown in Alaska. He explained what they were and how to grow them, indicating only the size and the shape of the seeds. He described each flower to come, each beauty. He relaxed as he talked. Seed by seed, the stutter-halt-stutter disappeared into an easy onesided conversation.

"Do you want some tea?" I offered when the silences between his statements lengthened again.

"I like tea," he said. "But I usually drink coffee."

Brian, who watched the exchange with a mildly surprised look on his face, looked back toward the TV screen and turned up the volume.

⁓

Erin's crime spree in December of 2007, three years after I had met him, was so sudden and violent that headlines in the paper described it as "26 Hours of Murder and Mayhem." At 5:30 a.m., Erin killed his sleeping father with a machete and attacked his father's fiancée, Elann Moren. Less than two hours later, Erin shot and killed Jason Wenger in an effort to steal his vehicle. But the shots made a lot of noise, so Erin fled on foot rather than risk a confrontation with one of Jason's neighbors. He rested in the woods near downtown. By

7:20 p.m., Erin was ready to kill again. When Elizabeth Rumsey walked past him on her way home, Erin asked her for the time. She testified later that she may have been "a little rude" to Erin, but there was something about his demeanor that unnerved her. He shot her in the back three times. Twenty-four hours after the first slaying, Erin wanted to kill more, as much as possible, anybody. When Tamas Deak went outside to start his car, Erin shot and maimed him as well, then took his SUV. Finally, twenty-six hours after Christopher Erin Rogers Sr. was hacked to death, and after a crosstown chase involving several collisions, the police took Erin into custody.

❧

While Elizabeth Rumsey waited for the paramedics after Erin shot her in the back, Signe Jorgenson, a fellow graduate student in Jason Wenger's creative writing program, walked alone across a dark parking lot and secluded side street to reach a classmate's apartment. The whole MFA program had come there, it seemed. They were in shock. Nobody knew what to do or say, just that they had to gather and meet up with the living. At that point, nobody knew who had killed Jason or that Erin was still hunting.

That night, as Signe walked back to her car, she thought of a piece Jason had shared in a nonfiction workshop they'd taken together. He had written of a job working with emotionally disturbed juveniles in Colorado. It was similar, in a way, to the kind of work he'd been doing in Anchorage. The essay was raw and rough around the edges but real. Just like Jason, she thought. Signe and Jason played on the same softball team. They could be losing by ten runs, but he'd congratulate every hit, every good play.

Signe wasn't Jason's closest friend, but he had a way of making everyone feel important. The next morning, she thought she was okay and went to the university's writing center where she worked as a tutor. But shock can make a person feel well or ready to get back to life when she should be taking some time. The news reports were sinking in.

"I lost it in the middle of a tutoring session," Signe says. "It was one of the most embarrassing moments of my life to date."

Signe may have realized that walking alone on that particular day was a game of roulette, or perhaps she hadn't understood until then that death can come to any of us, at any time. She may have simply been grieving for her friend. Shock, it seems, can be softer than it sounds, until it wears off.

ℯↄ

It's more than the brush against violence that horrifies the survivors of a psychopath and the families of the slain; it's the psychopath's absence of guilt. And it's not only the dead who haunt the living, but the questions, the betrayal: Was this meant to happen? What good God would let this happen? Could anyone have known? Intervened?

*I should have called him.*

*He should have slept in, turned left, stayed home. I should have held that child, hugged that child.*

The day after that Most Dangerous Day, Erin looked a lunatic, a madman baring his teeth for the news cameras at the arraignment. Remorse was not evident. It was clear in the dead-wild eyes that Erin had rent his humanity, and all that remained of him was elemental, an essential rage.

*Psykhe* is Greek for "mind" and *pathos* for "suffering." People once believed psychopaths were possessed by Lucifer. Psychopathy couldn't be human nature; it had to come from somewhere else. Erin said his mother, Scary Sherry, would slap him because he looked like his father—"Too late to enter the murky waters of family dynamics," the prosecutor said.

Psychopaths are characterized by specific personality traits like deceitfulness, lack of empathy and guilt, impulsiveness, and antisocial behavior. Most disturbing is the continuity of this aberrance in the human population, of which psychopaths have long been a stable proportion. And psychopathy has, according to researchers, a "substantial heritable component of 50 percent." Does psychopathy explain how a man, a son, can do what the rest of us cannot imagine, even at our angriest? Experts conclude that "the muting of the social emotions is the proximate mechanism that enables psychopaths to pursue their self-centered goals without feeling the pangs of guilt."

When does the muting happen? As a young adult? At twenty years old, Erin set two fires on the same day because he and a friend were "walking around bored." Arson, like animal torture, is a red flag for antisocial personality disorder. It would have been too late to intervene by then. But what about high school? Erin had graduated from the Alaska National Guard Youth Corps Challenge Program, designed to help "problem kids turn their lives around." Clearly that intervention had not worked. What about elementary school? Kindergarten? When wasn't it too late? Risk factors for antisocial behavior are environmental, genetic, and neurobiological; they can begin in the womb and continue throughout childhood.

I should say here that I'm not privy to Erin's psychological diagnosis, nor was his psychological state addressed at his trial. I did, however, meet his mother (another random coincidence). I was sixteen years old, working as a maid for the same lodge that employed Sherry. Her youngest son, Erin's brother, was my age, and he stayed with her in employee housing. I don't remember much of her, just a shrill tone, the way she belittled her boy in public, the way he pretended not to be bothered. Even then, in a roadside town with a population of three hundred, people started calling her Scary Sherry, like they knew.

*Risk begins in the womb and continues through childhood.*

To know where Erin's rampage originated, we would have to go back all the way, when Sherry and Chris Sr. had met, made love or something like it, and cells had divided in a common miracle. Messy. Exquisite. Erin ticked into existence, a countdown, T minus thirty or so years.

❧

Sometimes when I think about bombs, I think about Brian and the nature of events that constitute "muting of social emotions." I think of a love, long ago burned up, and a man I left speeding toward forty, steered by and still believing every terrible thing his dad said about him.

A piece of shit. That's what you are. Nothing.

The mind grows strong to contain the suffering. Until it can't.

❧

In 2007 I didn't know Christopher Erin Rogers Jr., the name all over the news and radio. But during the five o'clock broadcast of the arraignment, I recognized Erin. No longer a skinny, long-haired, shy guy, he looked feral, skinhead bald with an unkempt beard. Had he become addicted to meth? Wasn't there something, anything that could rationally explain it?

Brian called me that day. We hadn't spoken for a few months. "Crazy shit, huh?" he said. I said that I had thought Erin was a good guy, just lonely. I was wrong. I asked Brian if Erin had been on any heavy drugs.

"I don't know. Probably. I mean, he was out there," Brian said. Erin, Theo, and Brian had been roommates for a short time in 2005, after Brian and I broke up. We had two tumultuous years, and I think I would have gone on pretending things were fine if Brian hadn't professed interest in another woman, one closer to his age, who wouldn't count how many beers he drank or expect so much.

I had loaded my little red truck with all of Brian's things—the bed, bookshelves, kitchen appliances, tools—and given him one last ride to Theo's. Brian sat quietly in the passenger seat, staring out the window, staring at his hands, staring at the scars on his knee, never at me.

Erin was in the process of moving out when Brian moved in. Apparently, Erin had taken issue with Theo's housekeeping and had attacked him with a miniature Christmas tree that hadn't been put away by June. Erin went on hitting him even after Theo lost consciousness, and he may have continued the beating had Theo's dog not intervened. When Theo came to, he called the police. Erin called Animal Control. They agreed Erin would find a new residence.

When I dropped Brian off, it was not long after the incident. Wrappers and Taco Bell bags once again covered the lawn Erin had worked on. I parked on the street because in the driveway a blue Honda hatchback was rusting on four flat tires. The mailbox tilted away from Theo's house, away from the bare bay windows that reflected the street like a one-way mirror.

Brian walked up to the door with a box in his arm. The worn wood of the porch creaked. He hesitated, eyes twitching toward the Beware of Dog sign.

"I fucking hate that dog," he said.

"I don't blame you." I grabbed a box out of the truck's cab and followed him.

Theo's house was an olfactory assault, a bouquet of cigarette smoke and dog urine. Earlier that summer, Theo had caught a salmon and forgotten about it in the vegetable crisper until its juices puddled and dried on the floor beneath the fridge. Nicotine stains browned the ceiling tiles; several were missing, others sagged with moisture. A cluster of live wires hung from the ceiling fan. My eyes ran over urine streaks and gray smudges on the once-white walls to stop on crusty carpet strewn with empty Mickey's Ice 40s.

Was this the freedom Brian had been craving? I finished unloading his things and wished him well.

❧

In 2006, a year after he moved to the house in Spenard, Brian invited me to Theo's birthday party. Theo and I didn't like each other, but I wanted Brian to see how good I was doing on my own. I could have been doing homework or reading campy sci-fi novels, but the mind, sometimes, makes its own suffering, and my mind thought I was lonely for Brian.

I arrived around 9:00 p.m. and missed the crowd. The guests left early when Theo started shadowboxing. The house was in order.

Brian had shampooed the carpet and repainted the walls. All the fixtures had lightbulbs and all of the ceiling was tiled. When I walked into the living room, Brian was trying to end a drunken heart-to-heart.

"I'm just lonely, you know, man." Theo leaned forward on the tattered couch, his face wet and red, snot dripping from his nose.

"You've got to pull your shit together, man. You think some chick is going to hang out in your room? It's disgusting. You need to clean that shit up. Take a shower."

I watched from the periphery, thinking back to when I first met Theo. We had both worked swing shift at the Village Inn in 2003, my freshman year. Only three years had passed, but a few years of garbage partying makes a husk of a man. Theo was bloated and gray skinned. He had no family in Anchorage, and other than a few who would come around to share his beer and weed, he really had no friends. His paychecks disappeared within hours. Brian had told me that before Theo's girlfriend left him, he didn't drink very often and could get through a whole conversation without crying or starting an argument.

"I love you, Brian," Theo said. "I'm trying to be better." He cried artlessly, snorting and wheezing, whimpering. Brian looked at me for a moment, picked Theo up like a baby, and turned to take him to his room. When they reached the hallway, Brian accidentally knocked Theo's head into the wall.

"You fat motherfucker, watch where you're going!"

⁓

MAN CHARGED IN PAIR OF SEXUAL ASSAULTS
*Anchorage Daily News*, June 6, 2008

The first rape took place about midnight Wednesday, when the victim was returning to her camp from the portable toilets and was approached by a man she knew as Deuce, according to documents prosecutors filed in court. He lured her away with the offer of beer, then pushed her to the ground and began beating and raping her. Afterward, she ran to a nearby tent, then to the Black Angus Inn, to call police, who began their investigation.

Then, about 11:00 a.m., police got another nearly identical report of a rape in the same woods and set up a perimeter around the Sullivan Arena to begin a manhunt. They found Theadose Merculief (Theo) a short time later, still with blood on his hands.

Merculief is charged with three counts of first-degree sexual assault, one count of second-degree sexual assault, and two counts of fourth-degree assault. As Judge Brian Clark read the sentencing range for each count in court Thursday—up to ninety-nine years in prison for the first-degree sexual assaults—Merculief stared off with a resigned look on his face.

"You might as well send me away for the rest of my life," he said.

❧

Mercy, its common use, dates back to the twelfth century: "God's forgiveness of his creatures' offenses," from the Old French *merci*, a "reward, gift; kindness, grace, pity." It is the heavenly reward of those who show kindness to the helpless.

At Erin's sentencing hearing, Elann Moren, who saw and heard her fiancé being hacked to death by his own son, read her victim impact statement and implored the judge, "Your Honor, Christopher Erin Rogers Jr. butchered my heart, filleting it as surely as he slaughtered his father. Show him the same mercy he showed us."

The judge heard Moren. At the end of his last trial in January of 2010, Christopher Erin Rogers Jr., the man I knew only as Erin, was sentenced to a total of 498 years. His public defender said, "We're on the precipice, looking at sentencing a troubled young man to a greater composite sentence than Robert Hansen received for kidnapping, torturing, raping twenty-nine women and then taking them out in the bush, letting them loose, and hunting them down and killing them."

❧

Once Erin unleashed the machete, unsheathed the suffering, he wanted to kill more. He would have killed Elann Moren too. She huddled in the locked bathroom while Erin charged the door. For the second time, one of Erin's rampages was interrupted by a dog; this time Elann's. Erin fled the scene. He wanted to kill more. And more. It could have been anybody, the police said, but it was Jason on his last winter Sunday. It was a twenty-seven-year-old creative writing student. A man who worked for a nonprofit whose mission was to help the mentally ill. A believer. "He was a terrific guy who had overcome his own troubled days to become one of the most compassionate people I've ever known," said a mutual friend.

It could have been anyone. Where was I that morning? Spending my cash? As self-involved as any single twentysomething? It could have been me. The driver's side door to my truck didn't even lock. I sometimes sat inside the cab on winter mornings, on cold Sunday mornings, smoking a cigarette and drinking my coffee, suffering contained.

❧

In seventh grade I was asked to recite poetry, verses that are fused into my long-term memory and that, to this day, weave with my thoughts like lines of a radio song. Frost with his promises to keep, Hopkins and his Margaret relishing the blight, Blake's Tiger—Did He who made the lamb make thee? But the metaphor that attached most thoroughly to my preteen psyche emerged from a funeral poem, author unknown:

> Man's life is laid in the loom of time
> To a pattern he does not see
> While the weavers work and the shuttles fly
> Till the dawn of eternity.

It's an old metaphor, that the universe is woven, and that each life is a thread—some dark, some light, and all crucial to the Pattern. While the poem uses weavers in plural, it asserts that God, singular, surely planned the pattern:

He only knows its beauty,
And guides the shuttles which hold
The threads so unattractive,
As well as the threads of gold.

I didn't question this as a child. I believed. But these days it sounds more like a question than a certainty: Surely God planned this pattern? And if not God, who or what are the weavers?

It could have been anyone.

෴

Here's what strikes me about Jason Wenger and about Erin's "random" victims: they were gold threads, silver threads. Bright white, go to church Sunday morning, make a difference, jog to work, call your folks and let them know you're okay threads.

*One of the most compassionate people I've ever known.*

"I just wanted to kill a couple more people," Erin explained.

The prosecutor described Erin's crimes in their full gruesome truth during the first trial: Erin came into his father's bedroom and started "hacking" the couple. His father did his best to fight him off and to protect his fiancée. He shoved Erin out of the bedroom and into the kitchen. The father collapsed and died naked on the linoleum floor.

"This is how it happened," the prosecutor told the jury. "You're going to hear much more. You're going to see much worse. I should also tell you what I'm not going to prove—why he did this."

Erin's public defender agreed. "He's absolutely right about one thing: we're not going to figure out why."

Why not? Why hadn't Erin's defense attorney bothered to explain motive either? Or the press, who called him killer, hacker, hunter—who described a man who "yawned" at his morning ar- raignment? What if we could look at the pattern, see where the weave tightened, tightened, and threadbare, broke? Jason's parents believe his murder is God's choice, and they expressed as much at the funeral, but I cannot believe that there are no other interested parties. Don't his victims want to know why? Or Erin's family? Are we afraid of answers?

Look—a thread, a single strand that stretches both ways infinitely: here it is smooth as water, luminous and mysterious; there it is coarse as rope, fibers like splinters. Here is the father, slaughtered on the linoleum, and there is Sherry, her firstborn forming in her womb, and then the quickening, the quickening—the child stirs.

❧

When I was quite young, I asked my brother, then a teenager, what God was. As a son of a single, working mother, my brother was more like a parent than a sibling to me. He was surprised by my question, I think. That is, I clearly remember the expression on his face, and I understand now that he felt bad that I even had to ask. The following Sunday he loaded me into the little red wagon (he didn't drive yet), pulled me to the Assembly of God, and left me with the Sunday school class.

I learned of the Trinity, David and Goliath, and the Virgin Mary. I had a lot of questions, and the teacher kindly answered them, but it was all very confusing. What scared me most about this God was that He wouldn't let my cat come to heaven (I asked if I could bring her). How mean, I thought, and each night afterward I prayed over my cat, trying to convince God to change His no-animals-in-the-kingdom rule. God remained silent.

What made the experience so shocking, and why I remember praying and pleading for so many nights, is that it was my first time confronting what I saw as one of life's irreconcilable cruelties.

❧

I knew three men who shared a house in Spenard. Dark yarn, laced together. I don't know why I knew these men yet never knew Jason Wenger. I don't know why it hurt so much to lose Brian or why I let him break my heart, but I do remember the night Brian told me why he had stopped believing in God. It was after Erin went on the killing spree and before Theo became a rapist.

Brian had moved out of Theo's place and into an apartment building near mine. Sometimes he asked me to come over to keep him company. Brian was several months into sobriety, something he hadn't experienced since he was fourteen years old. I was the closest thing he had to a sponsor.

We were lying on top of his covers and staring at the ceiling. This was not a romantic situation; he had no furniture apart from his bed. That day he seemed sad.

"Why are you an atheist?" I asked out of the blue. Brian didn't want to join a traditional recovery program. He didn't like the religious overtones of the twelve steps.

"I didn't used to be," he said. "I remember knowing there was a God when I was a kid. I mean, I didn't get it from my parents. They weren't religious. But I just knew that I came from something."

"I don't get it."

"I mean, when I was a kid, I remember knowing there was something before all of this."

"What happened?" I asked.

"My Big Brother," he said. Brian never had a big brother but when he was thirteen years old, his mother put his sister into foster care and skipped town with her boyfriend, the man who had been molesting Brian's little sister. Brian moved in with his mentor from the Big Brothers Big Sisters program.

"Why? Was he an atheist?"

"No. He was a Christian. I never told you why I left."

"Didn't your dad come for you?" I thought I'd heard his history.

"No. He didn't ever come for me. *I* had to find *him*. After about a week my Big Brother started trying shit."

"What do you mean by shit?" I asked.

"Gay shit."

I didn't want him to have to tell me what happened next. Instead I asked, "What did you do?"

"I left. I stayed under a bridge for a little while. I went to my grandparents' house when I got hungry."

"But you stopped believing in God?"

He didn't say anything. We lay in the lamplight of his small room not looking at each other. His apartment building was jokingly referred to as Felony Flats because it was one of the only places that would rent to known criminals. I wanted to invite him back to my place, where I would be more comfortable, but he was already self-conscious about his environment. The silence stretched on, and I waited for Brian to finish his thought, but he seemed unwilling to say anymore.

"I think you did okay, you know?"

Brian didn't answer. Instead he pulled the silence over us, heavy and warm as a quilt. Soon his breathing was audible and even. He slept and I listened with my whole body. I listened and I believe that I am still listening to what I heard in his breath—giant shuttles of flowering dogwood flying across the Loom.

# TROUT, MOSTLY

He stands on the bridge by the university, pole in hand, black-and-white flannel, black T-shirt, denim trousers worn to a crust. I spot him after the morning lecture where students train to be keen to landscape, character, opposites. It would be insensitive to reach into my satchel and pull out a journal, to capture in a quick sketch the glorious way his mustache explodes outward. The brim of his soiled beige hat allows light and shadow to move across his flat features and red-leather skin. Sun-loved. He doesn't look city-born.

I once read that it's common for the urbanite to dream of farming during times of stress. Our collective memory reaches out with calloused hands, and we itch to milk cows or pitch bales of hay from a truck bed. As though part of our body is dormant in the knowledge it can grow or gather everything it needs. It's easy, at the day's end, to romanticize leaning against a porch rail with one last, satisfied look out at fields that slope into a fading golden sky.

I came from the country, granddaughter of a man who felled trees, built homesteads, came to town for salt and whisky. During his life I was embarrassed by his conversations and the gaminess of his sweat-soaked clothes. I recoiled from his coarse language and the unexamined practice of his social values, racism and sexism included. I was ashamed too of my own poverty and calluses. But this education—walking on cement, indoor plumbing, the boom of jets thrusting upward, the incessant speed of everything—pulls me toward the man on the bridge, who, like my kin, dangles live worms from a string. I want for us both to intimately know knots, not nominalizations, academia, the broad empty spaces between celestial bodies.

The break will not last long; soon there will be more lectures. I tap the man on his shoulder, compelled to ask the obvious: "You fishin'?"

"Sure am," he says.

"What runs in this? Didn't think there were fish here."

"Trout, mostly," he says, neither terse nor eager for conversation.

He tilts his head. His eyes follow the translucent fishing line though the pole's guides, and his quick fingers deftly tie on more bait. The worm looks like flesh against the high afternoon sun. But for the fact of the bridge, I may not have seen this creek, covered as it is by willow branches stretching bank to bank. The water eddies underneath, cold and clear.

"You look straight down, you'll see 'im there," he says. But everything under the flow is a single, bronze mudscape. My eyes have forgotten how to see, to differentiate the pebbles, silt, life—the tentacles of grass sliming into the current. I peer hard into the water and a memory flashes: I'm dangling my bare feet from the railroad trestle back home, watching fish jump from the murky green lake. The water smelled minerally, like blood or coins, subtle but strong enough to distinguish from the tar of the railroad ties or the forest hemming the lakeshore where I learned to fish. I smell it now, as distinct in my memory as bread or bacon.

"I just don't see it. I mean, I just can't see—"

"It's right there," he says, eyes flitting to the water.

"Why can't I see it?" I ask, feeling I have lost something important.

A tin can rests on the wooden rail. Inside, the bait coils and writhes. The man pulls out a worm, and it pushes its ends against the air, pushes because that is what a worm does with or without the earth hugging against it.

"Right there," he says. "Just look." He tosses the worm into the stream. "You see that yet?"

I don't.

"You watch this now. Look here." Another worm drops into the stream.

And there he is—a small gray fella, maybe four inches. All around him worms drop like rainbows, like pennies, like winged things.

"Catch and release?" I ask.

"Oh yeah. Too small to keep," he says.

On the other side of the bridge a sidewalk forks in two directions. One split leads from the university to the parking lot, the road, and every place I ever escaped. The other path dips into the woods, hugs the creek for a while, swims in and out of the campus structures, the hospital, extending west to the city. In my dreams, this bridge will merge with a trestle, and the creek will become a hundred other lakes and streams. On good nights I will dangle my feet and look to the sky, where the big empty spaces above the earth roil with everything we've forgotten.

# ACKNOWLEDGMENTS

My ultimate gratitude to the men and women who shared their stories and allowed me to peek into their lives and thoughts. Thank you, Cowboy and Lou and Rea. Thank you, Mark Coon. Thank you, Diana Waggy and all of the real women of Hiland—Nikki, Felisha, Nicole, Cassandra—meeting you and hearing your stories made my world better.

I owe more than I can ever repay to my faithful first reader. Thank you, Peter, for all the weekends when my projects came first, for changing diapers, for making dinner, and for teaching me something new every day. You are my anchor.

I am eternally thankful for the wonderful writing teachers who helped me with this manuscript and for all of their sound advice: Sherry Simpson, Nancy Lord, Ernestine Hayes, and Linda McCarriston. It's an honor to know you.

My hat off to Maranda Weis; the editorial staff at *Chautauqua* magazine; Victor Lavalle; Laura Julier, and the folks at *Fourth Genre* for your insights and editorial suggestions. I am equally grateful to the *Permafrost* magazine staff for their strong support of this book and for passing it along to University of Alaska Press.

Thank you, dear friends, who coaxed this work into the light: Erica Watson, Michael Dinkel, Deb Liggett, Marilyn Sigman, Lu-Anne Haukaas Lopez. And thank you, Signe Ellen and Peter, Raina, and Sara Graziano, for giving me encouragement when encouragement was what I needed the most.

Finally, I would like to gratefully acknowledge the magazines where these essays first appeared:

"Mercy," *Permafrost* 35, no. 1
"A History of Smoking," *Southampton Review* 11, no. 1

"Notes from a Baltic Avenue" appeared as "Good Neigh-
   bors," in *UAA Showcase Journal* 25
"Open Holds," *bioStories* 4, no. 1
"A Man of Fashion," *Alaska Quarterly Review* 30, nos. 3–4
"A Man of Fashion," excerpted under the title "Hard Walkin'
   Mark." *F Magazine* 3, no. 5
"The Real Women of Hiland Mountain," *Chautauqua* 12
"Stronghold," *Citron Review* (Winter 2013–14)
"The Origin of Light," *Alaska Quarterly Review* 34, nos. 3–4
"Threadbare," *Fourth Genre* 17.2
"Trout Mostly," *Vine Leaves* 16

Mary Kudenov was born in Haines, Alaska and moved between the Southeast and Kenai Peninsula, before settling in Anchorage for over a decade. She holds an MFA in Creative Writing and Literary Arts from the University of Alaska Anchorage, and her nonfiction has appeared in several literary magazines. Mary currently lives in North Carolina with her husband, Peter, and their son, David.